MINNA VON BARNHELM

GERMAN LITERARY CLASSICS
IN TRANSLATION
General Editor: KENNETH J. NORTHCOTT

Georg Büchner
LEONCE AND LENA; LENZ; WOYZECK
Translated by Michael Hamburger

Friedrich Hölderlin and Eduard Mörike
SELECTED POEMS
Translated by Christopher Middleton

J. M. R. Lenz
THE TUTOR and THE SOLDIERS
Translated by William E. Yuill

Gotthold Ephraim Lessing
MINNA VON BARNHELM
Translated by Kenneth J. Northcott

Friedrich von Schiller
WILHELM TELL
Translated by William F. Mainland

Gotthold Ephraim Lessing

MINNA VON BARNHELM
A Comedy in Five Acts

Translated
and with an
Introduction
by
KENNETH J.
NORTHCOTT

The University of Chicago Press
Chicago and London

The University of Chicago Press, Chicago 60637
The University of Chicago Press, Ltd., London

International Standard Book Number: 0–226–47341–4 (clothbound)
Library of Congress Catalog Card Number: 70–189867

CONTENTS

INTRODUCTION

The position of Gotthold Ephraim Lessing in the history of German literature and criticism is an assured one. In many senses we may agree with the critics that his works represent, if not the beginnings of modern German drama, at least the catalyst which preceded it. This catalytic function depends upon two complementary achievements, the first of which consists of the four great plays by which his imaginative writings are chiefly remembered: *Miss Sara Sampson* and *Emilia Galotti*, works which introduced the *bürgerliches Trauerspiel* or "domestic tragedy" to the German stage as a new genre; the verse drama *Nathan der Weise*, a virtual manifesto of the ideas of the enlightened tolerance of the eighteenth century; and *Minna von Barnhelm*, one of the few great comedies to be written for the German stage before the twentieth century. Three of these four plays show a high degree of eclecticism: Diderot and Lillo are acknowledged by Lessing as having influenced *Miss Sara Sampson* and *Emilia Galotti*, and the characterization in *Minna von Barnhelm* owes much to French and English models. Nevertheless, all of these plays have an innovative quality which makes them of special importance for the German stage, and they all reveal Lessing as a dramatist of high quality.

Lessing's second contribution to the drama goes beyond that of the practicing playwright. He was a prolific critic and theorist of the drama, and we should not forget, in this context, that he was the author of one of the major works of art criticism in the eighteenth century, *Laokoon*. In his capacity as critic and theorist, however, Lessing's main contribution probably has to be seen in his introduction of Shakespearean drama to the German stage. This is not to suggest that Shakespeare was unknown to German audiences prior to this time, but the efforts of the English troupes who had early brought his plays to the continent had led to a devaluation of the poetic nature of his drama and had laid emphasis on the sensationalism of, say, *Titus Andronicus*. This reevaluation of Shakespeare was to have the most far-reaching effects upon the development of German drama during the last decades of the eighteenth century and, consequently, upon later periods as well.

Lessing's critical writings are collected in three major works: the *Hamburg Dramaturgy* (*Hamburgische Dramaturgie*), written in the years 1767 to 1769; *Letters about the Latest Literature* (*Briefe die neueste Litteratur betreffend*), written between 1758 and 1760; and the virtually contemporaneous *Essays on Fable* (*Abhandlungen über die Fabel*). It is in the seventeenth of the letters on literature that Lessing makes his famous defense of Shakespeare and his attack upon neoclassical French drama, which had been so enthusiastically supported by Gottsched, whose heavy hand had had such an influence upon the German stage during the two preceding decades. Lessing's theoretical works on the drama are, like Aristotle's, more concerned with tragedy than comedy, and particularly with the interpretation of the key theme *heleos* and *phobos*. That we shall not deal with these at the present time is not because of any lack of importance but rather because they have no bearing upon *Minna von Barnhelm*. Before turning to the immediate consideration of our play, we must stress, as H. B. Garland has done, that without the pioneering work of Lessing, the whole literary movement of the Storm and Stress would have lacked a dramatic tradition on which to build, and the drama of this period, which formally and to some extent thematically employed the freedom of Shakespearean drama, with its rapid changes of mood, scene, and milieu, could not have developed as speedily as it did. However, this is not to suggest, as Garland points out, that Lessing was necessarily at one with the creations of his younger contemporaries.[1]

Some literary historians have taken the position that there was virtually no comic tradition on the German stage before *Minna von Barnhelm*, while others declare that the play is the first "examplary" German comedy. Like all generalizations, these viewpoints contain some elements of truth. The tradition of comedy, and of its companion form, farce, goes as far back as the vernacular scenes which were introduced into the early medieval passion plays. The tradition then develops through the Shrovetide plays until, in the hands of Hans Sachs, it reaches a true peak in the comedy both of character and of situation, though admittedly in plays of very small compass. Regrettably, the development ceased at this point, and the writings of Hans Sachs, which might well have represented a true beginning of a new era of dramatic productivity, proved to be no more than a dead end. The popular traditions of comedy in Germany, unlike their counterparts in English literature, did not contribute in any truly significant way to the continuing mainstream of German comic writing.

The seventeenth century saw three comedies by Andreas Gryphius, including *Peter Squenz*, an unsuccessful imitation of an incident in *A Midsummer Night's Dream*; but these were far removed from the

---

1. H. B. Garland's *Lessing, the Founder of Modern German Drama* (Cambridge: Bowes and Bowes, 1949) gives a sound introduction in spite of the broad claim implicit in the title.

direction of dramatic development in the first half of the sixteenth century. In fact the situation by the end of the seventeenth century had degenerated to such an extent that little comedy was performed which was not the broadest slapstick or the most exaggerated farce; and it was to this that Gottsched reacted by proclaiming the symbolic banishment of the traditional figure of Hans Wurst from the German stage, thus helping, in part at least, to lay the foundations of the myth that German comedy proper begins with *Minna von Barnhelm*.

It is true, on the other hand, that in contrast to the French and English dramatic traditions, German literature contains very few major comedies. Speculations on the reasons for this, though fascinating, inevitably lead to comparisons of national characters and in the end are likely to prove fruitless. Kleist's *Broken Jug (Der zerbrochene Krug)*, an examination of deceit in human behavior, is not far removed in spirit from his tragedies; Freytag's *The Journalists (Die Journalisten)* is pedestrian; and Grillparzer, Nestroy, and Raimund all belong to the Austrian tradition which largely reiterates elements from the comedies of the earlier periods. Probably the greatest comedy of the late eighteenth and early nineteenth centuries, and certainly one of the more theatrically effective, is Kotzebue's *The German Provincials (Die deutschen Kleinstädter)*, a brilliant literary lampoon on A. W. von Schlegel and at the same time a theatrically effective satire on the modes and manners of provincial life in the late eighteenth century. Goethe, however, disapproved of Kotzebue, and although the latter's influence on the theater in England and the United States was considerable in the nineteenth century, he remains unappreciated in his own country. Büchner's *Leonce and Lena* is the outstanding comedy of the nineteenth century, together with a work to which it owes a great deal, Tieck's *Puss in Boots (Der gestiefelte Kater)*.

The actual sources, both literary and personal, for the characters and situations in *Minna von Barnhelm* have been amply explored, and it will suffice to give a simple outline of them here.[2] *Minna von Barnhelm* was first published in 1767, that is, four years after the end of the Seven Years' War, but we know from Lessing's correspondence with his friend Ramler that he began the play in 1763, though it is likely that the bulk of the writing was done in 1766. In any case, there can be little doubt that Lessing's own involvement in the Seven Years' War, as the secretary of General Tauentzien, gave him an important insight into some of the problems with which the play is concerned. The character of Tellheim clearly owes a great deal to Lessing's close friend Ewald von Kleist, and incidental events of the play can also be traced to certain contemporary but somewhat peripheral historical events. There was, for example, a Major Marschall von Bieberstein, a Prussian like Tellheim, who loaned money to the Saxon authorities, and there are reports of one Werner who served as a general in the armies of Prince Heraclius and who rose to this position from the ranks. All these elements show that there is a great deal of local color, both historical and geographical, in the play.

It has already been pointed out that Lessing's theoretical writings show a greater involvement with tragedy than with comedy, but he does make certain important statements about the aim of comedy which have an important bearing on *Minna*. He believes, first, in the didactic aim of comedy, which is, he says, to teach by laughter but not by derision. "Every absurdity," he tells us in the twenty-eighth section of the *Hamburg Dramaturgy* (written in the same year that *Minna* was first published), "every contrast between

2. In his introduction to the German text published in 1965 (New York: St. Martin's Press), Garland goes into greater detail on this subject.

a defect and a reality is laughable. But laughter and derision are very far apart. We can laugh at a person, sometimes laugh about him, without in the least deriding him." (It will be important to view *Minna*, and especially the character of Tellheim, in the light of this statement.) He continues the contemplation of the nature of comedy in the next section of the *Dramaturgy*, where he says, "Its [comedy's] true and general use lies in laughter itself, in the exercise of our ability to notice what is laughable." When we have noticed what is laughable, in spite of all its possible disguises, then we shall know how to avoid being ridiculous ourselves, and this is the ultimate aim of comedy.[3]

If we bear all of these statements in mind, we may come to a closer understanding of Lessing's intentions in *Minna von Barnhelm*, though we may still, of course, question how successful he has been in carrying them out. It is the play itself which is of ultimate interest to us and not the search for putative sources which may indeed, if pursued to extremes, deny the dramatist the whole of his imaginative and inventive genius; but nevertheless we cannot entirely ignore the central historical background against which the play is set. This setting is a period of historical transition, not one of the great turning points of history, which Hebbel saw as the proper setting for tragedy, but one of those times when the individual, through force of circumstances, is driven to make a major readjustment in his personal life. The action occurs in the months immediately after the signing of the armistice between Prussia and Saxony, when the Prussian army is being disbanded and when the former members of those armies are faced with a major dis-

---

3. For a detailed treatment of the whole of Lessing's dramatic theories, the reader is directed to J. G. Robertson, *Lessing's Dramatic Theory* (Cambridge: Cambridge University Press, 1939), reprinted Bronx, N.Y.: Blom, 1965.

ruption of their lives and with uncertainty as to their future. It is a time when the individually well-ordered life of military discipline is being replaced by a life which for many will, initially, seem dreary and humdrum. Franziska is aware of this when she says to Minna:

Peace is supposed to make good all the evil caused by the war, but it also seems to destroy whatever good the war brought about. Peace ought not to be so obstinate, and anyway, how long have we been at peace? Time really drags when there is so little news. There's not much point in having the mails working again—nobody ever writes, because nobody has anything to write about. (act 2, scene 1)

Tellheim hints at the same possibility of boredom in his attempt to dissuade Werner from leaving to join Prince Heraclius:

A man should be a soldier in order to fight for his country or for a cause, not to serve here today and there tomorrow. That's no better than being a butcher's boy. (act 3, scene 7)

Characters find themselves in a state of turmoil and tension. Tempers flare easily. Werner cannot settle down; the landlord fears the possible decline in his earnings; Tellheim is torn between the demands made upon his heart by Minna and the restitution of his honor which he feels he has lost in a war that has also left him at least partially crippled. In such a situation it is not surprising that the objective dictates of reason may be superseded by behavior which, if not precisely irrational, may at times tend toward the exaggerated and hypersensitive. It is the treatment of these essentially individual and human problems in the main characters (and none of the characters is entirely free from them) which gives us an insight into Lessing's essential concern with the human condition. An armistice means that distinctions between human beings no longer depend upon which side a person is on, and that judgements of character can be made on the basis of human rather than political values.

Against this background, then, Lessing develops his comedy. By far the most difficult character in the play, and the one most frequently misunderstood, is Tellheim. Superficially, it may even seem that he is more suited to a tragedy than a comedy, or that he is distinguished from a Tartuffe or a misanthrope only by a deus ex machina in the shape of the intervention of the Count of Bruchsal in the final act. To take this view is to oversimplify the whole action of the play. Garland has rightly suggested that Tellheim is, indeed, not the rigid and unbending character that he is often made out to be, but rather a character who shows considerable inconsistencies. He is willing to change his point of view in an instant when he believes that his beloved Minna is threatened by poverty or disinheritance on his account. Love and compassion are shown to be more important to him than the honor of which he speaks so frequently; indeed, this desire for honor may have a measure of superficiality to it, for as Franziska says:

People very seldom talk about the virtues they have, but all the more frequently about the ones they don't have. (act 2, scene 1)

Minna immediately applies this to Tellheim, who in the past, apparently, has not been given to extolling any virtue but thrift. This Minna feels is a reflection of his tendency toward spendthrift habits. We may, then, see in this inner inconstancy to himself a reflection of the constancy which he shows toward Minna. In contrast to Tellheim, Werner presents a character who, though facing the same problems, is much more consistent. His straightforwardness, his absolute loyalty, and his generosity, together with his tender affection for Franziska, all serve to throw into relief the greater complexities and fragilities of Tellheim's character. Nevertheless, if we apply Lessing's own yardstick of laughter, we do find that we can laugh at Tellheim and at the ironies which surround him even in the complicated matter of the rings, but we never deride him, for the very reason that Lessing has placed him in a situation which has to call forth our sympathy. At the same time, in drawing Minna as so certain and secure a character, Lessing has provided us with a constant assurance that all will work out well in the end. We never doubt that Minna is sovereign in the situation, and our interest merely becomes focussed upon the "when" and not the "how" of the ultimate solution. Our assurance is made doubly sure because Minna never herself doubts that she can and will remain in control of the situation, even when she seems to have gone too far, and even at the point when she may begin to have some fleeting doubts; we have seen enough to know that the match will be made. In these circumstances the arrival of the Count of Bruchsal, for which, incidentally, we have been prepared throughout the play, becomes merely a confirmation of what we have known all along will come about, and not a sudden or inexplicable twist of fortune at the end, which will unite the lovers. Tellheim, then, is not a Molière character in whom an excess of human folly is probed and laid bare, but an honest man struggling to maintain his honesty in circumstances that are constantly conspiring against him. The lesson which Minna sets out to teach him by tricking him with the rings and by acting out a comedy within the play, which has itself a marked didactic purpose, is that he must not fear to reveal his essential humanity whatever the apparent hindrance. Tellheim must learn to trust others and not try to manipulate his world entirely on his own.

We have already spoken of Werner's humanity and his function in the play as a foil to Tellheim's complexity, but what of Franziska? If there is a resemblance between

Werner and Minna in their flexibility and sympathy for human weakness, there is a contrapuntal similarity between Franziska and Tellheim, though Franziska is a much more straightforward character than the major. Franziska reveals a humanity that is simpler than that of her mistress. She does not penetrate to the fundamental human purpose of Minna's plot against Tellheim. In Franziska's eyes it merely seems that Minna is playing with Tellheim, merely being cruel, and so she is very reluctant to be a party to the deception. Franziska, in her inflexibility, has her lesson to learn as well as Tellheim: she is too prone to see the world in terms of black and white and to judge people by their external appearances. Her discomfiture at the hands of Just when he outlines the fate of the servants with whom Franziska has been acquainted, and her oversimplified reaction to Riccaut de la Marlinière show that she has far too little real understanding of the mainsprings of human action.

The action of the play is centered on these four major characters, and it is symbolic of the characters that the love affair between Franziska and Werner meets none of the obstacles that beset that of Minna and Tellheim. The minor characters of the play, Just, the landlord, and Riccaut, fill out the comedy. The persistent state of hostility which exists between Just and the landlord allows Lessing ample opportunity for comic interludes, and certainly the drinking scene in the first act is one of the comic highlights of the play. Again we have a contrasting pair of characters. The landlord is a caricature of a grasping innkeeper, high-handed or cringing, depending upon what he believes to be the financial potential of his guest. The landlord also permits Lessing to introduce the satirical scene on police regulations in Berlin (which is presumably the town in which the action takes place). Just, by contrast, is the simple, gruff servant trying, with dog-like loyalty, to protect his master; it is not for nothing that Lessing puts the story of the poodle into Just's mouth, allowing him thus to characterize himself. As we have seen, Just also serves a didactic function in relation to Franziska, for he has none of the panache which the other servants display, but is an honest man, and in one sense at least, this is what the play is all about.

Riccaut de la Marlinière presents a more difficult problem of interpretation. On the basis of the introduction of this character, *Minna von Barnhelm* has sometimes been said to be the first drama which serves the cause of German nationalism. This was a notion which grew up in the nineteenth century when German literature frequently served or aided the nationalistic aspirations of the country. It is hard to believe that the man who wrote *Nathan der Weise*, with its great pleas for tolerance, and who infused *Minna von Barnhelm* with such gentle humanity would really have tried to turn it by this one comic and exaggerated character into a nationalist drama. The explanation must lie elsewhere. There is a difference between introducing a comic foreigner into a comedy and making an attack upon the whole nation of which that character is a single representative. It is, moreover, not out of the question that Lessing is making an attack upon the acceptance of French modes and manners by the Prussians, and especially Frederick the Great. These are legitimate ends but are not to be confused with jingoism. Riccaut, too, serves the function of allowing Lessing to show an important distinction between the characters of Minna and Franziska. Minna shows a greater maturity and insight in her evaluation of the true character of Riccaut. Whereas Franziska sees only the cheat, Minna sees the underlying insecurity of the man and sees that his vanity is merely a cover for this insecurity. At the same time, it must be pointed out that Minna's judgement may be clouded to some extent by her joy at receiving the news which Riccaut has brought her.

It is then another mark of the gentleness of Lessing's comedy that even the "bad" characters, those who show the more base human follies, are not really held up to ridicule. No disaster will befall Riccaut, and the landlord will, no doubt, continue to run his inn.

There is one further character of importance who has yet to be mentioned, and that is the widow Marloff. This small role is of importance because it is an example of a favorite device of the eighteenth-century theater in Germany: the introduction of the so-called cameo part. The part itself would generally be played by one of the leading members of the company, and it usually presented opportunities for a virtuoso performance *in nuce*. The scene has no influence upon the action of the play, though it does serve to underline the essential trait of generosity in Tellheim's character.

In spite of Lessing's espousal of the Shakespearean forms of the drama and his eloquent advocacy of them against the neoclassical forms, he maintains in his major plays the basic principles of dramatic unity which Shakespeare had in his practice rejected. *Minna von Barnhelm* is no exception. The total action of the play takes place in one day, during the hours of daylight, from Just's waking up in the morning until the arrival of the Count of Bruchsal in the afternoon. There is no change of scene during an act; and even when the scene does change at the end of an act, the change is only between two adjacent rooms. The action, simple as it is, is completely unified in Minna's determination to rehabilitate Tellheim and, in the parallel and equally straightforward wooing of Franziska by Werner.

Lessing constructs his play with great economy, and the exposition called forth high praise from Goethe on at least two occasions in his conversations with Eckermann.

On 26 July 1827 he told Eckermann: "The exposition of Lessing's *Minna von Barnhelm* is . . . excellent," and again on 27 March 1831 he said at greater length and with greater enthusiasm: "You may imagine how the play [*Minna von Barnhelm*] affected us young people as it suddenly emerged from that period of darkness. It was, truly, like a glowing meteor . . . . The first two acts are a masterpiece of exposition, from which we learned a great deal and from which we still can learn. It is true that nowadays no one wants to hear the word 'exposition,' and the effect which we used to await in the third act is now sought in the first scene. People forget that poesy is like sailing. You have first to push off from the shore and wait until you are some distance from it before hoisting full sail."

There can be no doubt of the validity of Goethe's assessment. In the space of the first two acts, or more precisely by the end of act 2, scene 6, we are in possession of all the details that we need to know about the main characters. We have been made privy to their strengths and weaknesses; we know their hopes and their intentions; and we know other people's opinions of them. Lessing himself was very concerned about the function of dramatic exposition and the mode of presenting characters to the audience. In the ninth section of the *Hamburg Dramaturgy* he says:

It is quite proper in everyday life not to nurse any offensive mistrust of another, and to give full credence to the witness which honest people bear to one another. But is the dramatic poet permitted to make use of this rule of fairness? Certainly not, even if he can make his task a very simple one by so doing. On the stage we want to see who people are, and we can only see this by their deeds. The good qualities that we are supposed to ascribe to them merely on the word of others can not possibly make us interested in them; it leaves us completely indifferent, and if we have no trace of personal experience of the characters, it even reacts badly upon those characters whose honesty and faith we are supposed to accept.

Lessing goes on to elaborate his theory by pointing out that in the course of twenty-four hours all the essentials of a character can be revealed not by majestic actions but by everyday deeds. All of this is admirably true of *Minna von Barnhelm*. We have a feeling of intimacy and deep knowledge of the characters, and part of our sense of well-being and security in the ultimate outcome of the play derives from our confidence in them. After such an exposition, Lessing can "hoist full sail"; the action proceeds from this point without interruption until the end of the play, except for a brief moment before the entry of the Count of Bruchsal.

To a modern audience, and especially one nurtured in the traditions of the English-speaking stage, the play may seem wordy, though the architectonics of it can scarcely be called into question. The plot may seem too slight to sustain so lengthy a treatment, and the device of the exchange of the rings, confusing and contrived. This, as we shall see, is not a reaction only of our own day. As a practical matter for production, judicious cutting may be permissible, and since we work with different traditions, the cameo part may be excised with little harm to the actual plot. We do have to understand, however, something about the acting traditions of the German stage in order to appreciate what Lessing is doing. The German theater from the seventeenth century to the twentieth has tended, even in periods of experiment, to be a theater in which the actor declaims. It is theater which has consistently relied more on the word than the action to sustain the interest of the audience and in which declamation was felt to be the basis of the actor's art. The simple fact that in many German theaters the prompter still reads every single word of the play half a line ahead of the actors reveals the importance which is attached to the text. There is still a great element of declamation on the German stage today, far more than would be acceptable to an English-speaking audience. Thus the word, in spite of Lessing's interest in Shakespeare and the short-lived innovations of the Storm and Stress dramatists, has essentially remained sovereign in the German theater. This fact has to be borne in mind if we are to avoid doing violence to the play by removing from it an essential quality and an element of leisureliness fundamental to its totality and unity.

Minna von Barnhelm still enjoys a great popularity on the German stage, and it was one of the first German plays to be adapted for the English theater. It was first presented in 1786 in a version by J. Johnstone called *The Disbanded Officer, or the Baroness of Bruchsal*. The title shows, however, the direction in which the dramatic interest lay and the importance which was ascribed to Tellheim. What is perhaps more important is that, with this version of *Minna*, there began a real interest in the German theater in England, though *The Disbanded Officer* was not, as has been claimed, the first German play to be performed there. Allardyce Nicoll records that Klopstock's little-known play, *The Death of Adam*, had been translated over twenty years earlier, in 1763, by R. Lloyd.[4] It was Johnstone's version of the present play, quickly followed by Schiller's *Robbers* and other plays of the Storm and Stress, however, which opened the gates to a flood of translations from the German and prepared the way for the great popularity which Kotzebue was to enjoy in the nineteenth century.

Minna von Barnhelm was adapted twice more in a relatively short period, once in 1799 by an anonymous translator, and once by Thomas Holcroft and his daughter in 1805. The Holcroft translation is published

---

4. Allardyce Nicoll, *A History of English Drama, 1660–1900*, vol. 3, *Late Eighteenth-Century Drama, 1750–1800* (Cambridge: Cambridge University Press, 1952), pp. 61–62.

in volume 2 of the *Theatrical Recorder* under the title *Minna von Barnhelm*, but already there was a feeling that it was too long for the English audiences, and Holcroft in a note on the play says:

This comedy has been so often declared by the Germans the best in their language, that I was determined to give it to the readers of the *Theatrical Recorder*, which work is intended to be the receptacle of excellence. That it has numerous masterly strokes of passion, and some of humor, and that the author well understood the best feelings of the heart, is true, and to his honor. But passion itself is here verbose: it almost wearies, yet the translation has been freely curtailed by my daughter and myself. . . . the Germans themselves, it is hoped, will not complain of the present version. . . . Apology for having occasionally omitted passages is scarcely necessary; this a German only will blame.[5]

The Holcrofts cut out the scene with Riccaut as "superfluous," thus destroying one of the great comic moments of the play, but doubtless the early nineteenth century looked for actions rather than words.

The present version has not been cut, and in its entirety it must stand as one of the major literary productions of the German Enlightenment, of the literature of which Lessing is, without doubt, the most illustrious representative.

5. Thomas Holcroft, *The Theatrical Recorder*, vol. 2 (London, 1806), p. 260. This and the first volume contain a number of articles on the history of the German stage and its contemporary state.

MINNA VON BARNHELM

PERSONS

MAJOR VON TELLHEIM

MINNA VON BARNHELM

COUNT OF BRUCHSAL, her uncle

FRANZISKA, her maid

JUST, Tellheim's servant

PAUL WERNER, former sergeant major in Tellheim's battalion

LANDLORD

LADY IN MOURNING

ORDERLY · SERVANTS

RICCAUT DE LA MARLINIÈRE

The scene alternates between two adjacent rooms of an inn.

ACT ONE

SCENE ONE

JUST, *seated in a corner, sleeping and talking in his sleep.* Bugger of a landlord . . . you . . . us ? . . . On guard! (*He goes through the motions of drawing his sword and in doing so wakes himself up.*) Bah! I can't even close my eyes without getting into a fight with him. I wish he'd been on the receiving end of half the blows I've dealt him . . . (*Yawns.*) But it's light out, I've got to find the master. As far as I'm concerned, he'll not set foot in this damn house again. I wonder where he spent the night.

SCENE TWO

JUST *and* LANDLORD

LANDLORD. Good morning, Herr Just, good morning. You're up early, or should I say you're still up so late?

JUST. You can say what you damn well like.

LANDLORD. I wasn't saying anything but "Good morning," and surely, Herr Just, you ought to say "Thank you" to that.

JUST. Thanks.

LANDLORD. Everyone feels a bit touchy when they don't get their proper rest. But never mind. So the major didn't come in last night, and you waited up for him?

JUST. You're clever, you are.

LANDLORD. Just guessing, Herr Just, just guessing.

JUST, *turning and about to leave.* Your servant, sir!

LANDLORD. Oh no, Herr Just, no!

JUST. All right then, I'm not your servant.

LANDLORD. Herr Just, I do hope that you're not still angry about yesterday. You shouldn't let the sun go down on your wrath, you know.

JUST. Well, I do and I shall let it go down on it till doomsday.

LANDLORD. Now, I ask you, is that Christian?

JUST. It's just as Christian as throwing an honest man out of the house because he can't pay his rent on the dot.

LANDLORD. Well, now, who could be so godless as to do a thing like that?

JUST. A Christian landlord . . . To think the master, a man like that, an officer of his stamp!

LANDLORD. And I'm the one who's supposed to have thrown him out of the house into the street? I'm afraid I have too much respect for officers to do that, and in any case too much sympathy with one who's just been discharged. I was obliged to ask him to move into another room, that's all—because of an emergency. Think no more about it, Herr Just. (*Shouts offstage.*) Hey there! I'll make it up to you in another way. (*Enter* SERVANT.) Bring us a glass. Herr Just would like a drop of something special.

JUST. Don't bother. Anything you offered me would turn to gall in my mouth. By God . . . No I mustn't blaspheme, I'm still sober.

LANDLORD, *to* SERVANT *who enters carrying a bottle of liqueur and a glass.* Give it to me. All right, you can go! Now, Herr Just, here's a drop of something special; strong, but gentle, and it'll do you good. (*Fills the glass and offers it to* JUST.) Just the thing for a stomach that's been up all night.

JUST. Well, I shouldn't really . . . but why should I sacrifice my good health to his bad manners? (*Takes the glass and drinks.*)

LANDLORD. Your health, Herr Just.

JUST, *giving him back the glass.* Not bad, but it doesn't make you any less of a scoundrel.

LANDLORD. Now, what about another quick one? You can't balance properly on one leg.

JUST, *having drunk the second glass.* Well, I must admit it's good, very good . . . homemade, of course?

LANDLORD. Not likely, real Danziger Goldwasser!

JUST. Now look here, landlord, if something like this could make me play the hypocrite, I would; but I can't, and so I tell you straight to your face—you're a scoundrel.

LANDLORD. That's the first time in my life that anyone ever called me that. Another one, Herr Just, all good things come in threes.

JUST. All right (*Drinks.*) Hm. Good, *very* good, but so is the truth . . . Truth's a good thing too . . . Landlord, you're a scoundrel.

LANDLORD. Now, I ask you, if I was a scoundrel, would I be standing here listening to you call me one?

JUST. Yes, you would. Scoundrels seldom have any guts.

LANDLORD. Won't you have another one, Herr Just? A four-stranded rope holds better, you know.

JUST. No, enough is enough. Besides, what's the use? If I drank the bottle down to the last drop, I wouldn't change my mind. Ugh, such a good drop of Danziger and such rotten manners. Throwing out a man like the master, who's lived here day and night and spent many a pretty penny here; throwing him out just because he wasn't spending quite as much—and behind his back into the bargain.

LANDLORD. But I needed the room. It was an emergency, and I knew the major would gladly have left it of his own free will if only we could have waited until he got back. Was I to turn a stranger away? I ask you. Was I to shove the trade down another landlord's throat? And besides, I don't think they could have found another place to stay. All the places are full up at the moment. You shouldn't have wanted a lovely young lady like that to have to stay out in the street. No, Herr Just, your master's too much of a gentleman to allow that. Besides, what does he stand to lose? Didn't I move him into another room?

JUST. Yes, right behind the pigeon loft . . . with a nice view between the chimneys of the houses next-door . . .

LANDLORD. Well, the view was all right until they started building. The rest of the room's nice enough—and it's got wallpaper.

JUST. You mean it had.

LANDLORD. It still has on one side. And you've got your little room next door, Herr Just . . . what's wrong with your room? There's a fireplace . . . well, perhaps it does smoke a bit in the winter . . .

JUST. But it looks all right in the summer . . . You're not trying to needle us, are you?

LANDLORD. Now, now, Herr Just, Herr Just . . .

JUST. Don't you get Herr Just excited, or else . . .

LANDLORD. Me? Get you excited? . . . No, that's the Danziger.

JUST. An officer like my master. Or perhaps you reckon that a discharged officer isn't an officer and couldn't break your neck. I wonder why you landlords were always such a help in the war. Every officer was an honest chap then. Does a bit of peace make you so cocksure?

LANDLORD. Now what are you getting angry about, Herr Just?

JUST. I want to get angry . . .

SCENE THREE

TELLHEIM, LANDLORD, *and* JUST

TELLHEIM, *entering.* Just!

JUST, *thinking it is the landlord who is talking to him.*
Just? Oh, so we're on those terms now, are we?

TELLHEIM. Just!

JUST. I thought I was Herr Just to you.

LANDLORD, *becoming aware of* TELLHEIM'*s presence.*
Sh! Sh! Herr Just, Herr Just . . . Look behind you . . .
your master.

TELLHEIM. Just, I believe you're quarrelling. What did
I tell you?

LANDLORD. Quarrel, Your Grace? Would I, Your Grace's
most humble servant, take it upon myself to quarrel
with one who has the honor to be in Your Grace's
service?

JUST. I'd like to give that humbug what for.

LANDLORD. It's true that Herr Just was speaking out on
behalf of his master . . . perhaps a little heatedly, but
he was right to do so. I think all the more of him for it;
in fact I admire him for it.

JUST. It's a wonder I don't knock his teeth down his
throat.

LANDLORD. It's really a shame, getting upset over
nothing. I'm as sure as can be that Your Grace would
not bring any disgrace on me for what I have done . . .
because it was necessary, because I had to.

TELLHEIM. Enough, sir. I owe you money. You moved
me out of my room in my absence. You must be paid.
I have to find somewhere else to stay. It's perfectly
understandable.

LANDLORD. Somewhere else? You're moving out, sir?
Oh, what a wretch I am! No, never! I'd sooner have
the lady moved out. The major can . . . well . . . if you
don't want to give her your room . . . the room's yours.

She'll have to go. I can't help it. I'll see to it at once,
Your Grace.

TELLHEIM. My friend, please do not do two stupid things
instead of one. The lady must, of course, retain
possession of my room.

LANDLORD. And to think that Your Grace thought I
mistrusted you, thought I was worried about my
money! As if I didn't know that Your Grace could pay
whenever he wanted to! That sealed purse with the
five hundred talers in it which Your Grace left in the
desk . . . Don't worry, it's in good hands.

TELLHEIM. I hope so—like the rest of my things. Just
will take charge of them when he pays the bill.

LANDLORD. Honestly, Your Grace, I was quite scared
when I found that purse. I always thought you were
an orderly and careful man, who wouldn't allow
himself to run out of money. But, well, if I'd really
thought that there was money in the desk . . .

TELLHEIM. You would have been a little more polite
with me.

LANDLORD. But Your Grace . . .

TELLHEIM. Come, Just, this gentleman is apparently not
going to permit me to tell you what to do, while we
are in his house.

LANDLORD. I'm going, Your Grace! My whole establish-
ment is at your service.

SCENE FOUR

TELLHEIM *and* JUST

JUST, *stamping his foot and spitting on the ground.* Pah!

TELLHEIM. What's the matter?

JUST. I'm fairly choking with rage!

TELLHEIM. That's about the same as having a plethora.

JUST. And you, sir, I just don't know you any more. Let
me die before your very eyes if you aren't the guardian

angel of this cunning, this merciless, dog. In spite of the gallows, in spite of the sword and the wheel, I'd have strangled him with my own hands and torn him to pieces with my own teeth.

TELLHEIM. Animal!

JUST. I'd rather be an animal than be like that.

TELLHEIM. What do you want?

JUST. All I want is for you to understand how they're insulting you.

TELLHEIM. And then?

JUST. I want you to have your revenge on him. But no! No, this fellow's not worth your bothering with.

TELLHEIM. Would you rather I told you to avenge me? That was my first thought. I hadn't intended him to see me again, and he was to receive his payment from you. I know that you can toss away a handful of money with a pretty disdainful gesture.

JUST. Ha! Ha! That would have been a good way of paying him off.

TELLHEIM. But one which I'm afraid we shall have to put off for the time being. I haven't a penny of ready money, and I don't know how to get any.

JUST. No ready money? What about that little purse with the five hundred talers which the landlord found in your writing desk?

TELLHEIM. That is money which was given to me to keep.

JUST. Not the five hundred talers which your old sergeant major, Paul Werner, brought you four or five weeks ago?

TELLHEIM. The very same. They belong to Paul Werner; why not?

JUST. You mean to say you haven't used them yet? You can do what you like with them, sir; I'll take responsibility.

TELLHEIM. Really?

JUST. I told Werner how long the paymaster general was taking to put your demands to rights. He heard . . .

TELLHEIM. That I would certainly be reduced to beggary, if I weren't already. I'm very grateful to you, Just. And this piece of news permitted Werner to share his bit of poverty with me. I'm glad to have got to the bottom of it. Now listen to me, Just; give me your bill as well; our partnership is at an end.

JUST. Eh? What?

TELLHEIM. Quiet! Someone is coming.

SCENE FIVE

A LADY IN MOURNING, TELLHEIM, *and* JUST

LADY. I beg your pardon, sir.

TELLHEIM. Who are you looking for madam?

LADY. Simply the worthy man with whom I have the honor to be speaking. You do not recognize me any longer. I am the widow of your former captain.

TELLHEIM. For heaven's sake, madam, but you are changed.

LADY. I have just risen from my sick-bed to which I had retired because of my sorrow at my husband's death. I am sorry to have to bother you so early, Major Tellheim. I am going to the country where a good-natured, though not exactly fortunate, friend has offered me a haven.

TELLHEIM, *to* JUST. Go, leave us alone.

SCENE SIX

LADY IN MOURNING *and* TELLHEIM

TELLHEIM. Speak freely, madam. You have no need to be ashamed of your misfortune in my presence. Can I be of service to you in any way?

LADY. Major . . .

TELLHEIM. I sympathize with you, madam. How can I be of service to you? You know that your husband was my friend—I repeat, my friend; and this is a title with which I have always been very sparing.

LADY. Who knows better than I how well he deserved your friendship and how well you deserved his? You would have been his last thought, your name the last word to escape his lips, had the ties of nature not reserved that right for his unfortunate son and for his unfortunate wife . . .

TELLHEIM. Enough. Madam! I would gladly weep with you, but today I have no tears. Spare me. You come upon me at a moment when I might easily be led to rail against Providence. O, my honest Marloff! Quickly, madam, what is your command? If I am in a position to help you . . . if I am . . .

LADY. I may not leave without fulfilling his last wish. He remembered just before his end that he was dying in your debt and made me swear to discharge this debt with the first money that I should receive. I sold his equipment, and I have come to redeem his note.

TELLHEIM. I beg your pardon, madam, it is for this that you have come?

LADY. For this. Please let me pay you the money.

TELLHEIM. Madame, I beg you. Marloff owed me money? That can scarcely be so. Let me see. (*Takes out his notebook and looks at it.*) I see nothing here.

LADY. You must have mislaid his note, and in any case, the note has nothing to do with it. Permit me . . .

TELLHEIM. No, madam, I am not in the habit of mislaying things of that sort. If I do not have it, then that is evidence that I never had it, or that it was cancelled and returned to him.

LADY. Major Tellheim!

TELLHEIM. Most certainly, madam. Marloff owed me

nothing. In fact I cannot even recall that he was ever in my debt. On the contrary, madam, I regard myself as having been left in his debt. I have never been able to pay off my debts to a man who for six years shared my happiness and my misfortune, my honor and my danger. I shall not forget that he has left a son. He shall be my son as soon as I can be his father. The confusion in which I find myself at the moment . . .

LADY. Generous man! But please do not think too lowly of me. Take the money, Major Tellheim; in this way I shall at least be put at ease.

TELLHEIM. What do you need to set you at ease, beyond my assurance that this money does not belong to me? Or do you want me to steal from my friend's infant and fatherless child? Steal, madam, that's what it would be in the truest meaning of the word. The money belongs to him, and you should invest it for him.

LADY. I understand you; please forgive me if I have not yet learned to accept favors. But how did you know that a mother will do more for her son than for her own life? I am going now . . .

TELLHEIM. Go, madam, go. Farewell. I shall not ask you to send me news of yourself, for such news might come at a time when I could make no use of it. But I forgot one thing, madam. Marloff still had money owing him from our former regiment. His demands are just as valid as my own. If mine are met, then his will be too. My word on it.

LADY. Sir . . . No, I would rather say nothing . . . To grant future favors is, in God's eyes, to have granted them already. I give you my thanks and my tears. (*Exit.*)

SCENE SEVEN

TELLHEIM

TELLHEIM. Poor woman! I must not forget to destroy that note. (*Takes some papers from his wallet and tears them up.*) Who can guarantee that my own need might not one day make me put them to use?

SCENE EIGHT

JUST *and* TELLHEIM

TELLHEIM. Are you there?

JUST, *wiping his eyes.* Yes.

TELLHEIM. You have been crying?

JUST. I have been writing out my bill in the kitchen, and the kitchen is full of smoke. Here it is.

TELLHEIM. Give it to me.

JUST. Have a bit of mercy on me, sir. I know people don't have much on you, but . . .

TELLHEIM. What do you want?

JUST. Well, I'd expected to die before getting the sack from you.

TELLHEIM. I have no further use for you. I have now to learn how to look after myself without servants. (*Opens the bill and reads.*) "The major owes me: three and a half months pay at six talers per month—twenty-one talers. From the first of the month I have paid out the following sums for him: one taler, seven groschen, nine pfennigs. Sum total, twenty-two talers, seven groschen, nine pfennigs." Just, I think I should pay you for the whole of the current month.

JUST. Look at the other side first, would you, major?

TELLHEIM. There's more? (*Reads.*) "I owe the major! Advanced on my account to the surgeon, twenty-five talers. For board and lodging during my convalescence, thirty-nine talers. Advanced to my father, whose house was burned and plundered, not to mention the two horses which he gave him, fifty talers. Sum total, 114 talers. Deduct the twenty-two talers, seven groschen, nine pfennigs brought forward: I remain in the major's debt to the tune of ninety-one talers, sixteen groschen, three pfennigs." Just, you're mad!!

JUST. I'm ready to believe that I've cost you a great deal more than that, but it would have been a waste of ink writing any more down. I can't pay you; and if you want to take my uniform away from me, which I also haven't paid for, then I'd rather you'd let me kick the bucket in some field hospital.

TELLHEIM. What do you take me for? You don't owe me anything, and I'll give you a recommendation to one of my friends who will look after you better than I can.

JUST. I don't owe you anything, yet you still want to throw me out.

TELLHEIM. Because I don't want to owe you anything.

JUST. Oh, just because of that? As sure as I know that I'm in your debt, I'm just as sure you don't owe me a penny, and just as sure that you shan't throw me out. You can do what you like, major, I'm going to stay with you, I've got to stay with you.

TELLHEIM. And your obstinacy, your defiance, your wild and impetuous conduct against everyone who you think has no right to interfere with you, your malicious spite, your desire for revenge . . .

JUST. You can paint me as black as you like, I won't think any worse of myself than of my dog. One evening last winter, in the twilight, I was walking along the canal and heard something whining. I climbed down, reached toward the voice, thinking that I was rescuing a child, and pulled a poodle out of the water. Well, that's all right too, I thought. The poodle followed me. Now I don't particularly like poodles. I chased him away, but it was no use. I beat him, but it was no use. I refused to let him into my room at night; he stayed in front of the door all night. If he got too close to me, I gave him a kick; he yelped, looked at me, and wagged his tail. I've never given him a thing to eat, but I'm the only one he obeys and the only one who can touch him. He runs along in front of me and does his tricks for me without being asked. He's an ugly poodle, but a very good dog. If he goes on like this, I'll have to stop disliking him.

TELLHEIM, *aside.* Exactly as I am to him! No, there *are* no completely inhuman people . . . Just, we'll stay together.

JUST. Certainly! . . . And you wanted to get on without a servant? You forget about your wounds and that you've only got the use of one arm. You can't get dressed by yourself. You can't do without me, and . . . not wishing to praise myself . . . and I am a servant, who . . . if worst comes to worst . . . can beg and steal for his master.

TELLHEIM. Just, we are not staying together.

JUST. All right!

SCENE NINE

SERVANT, TELLHEIM, *and* JUST

SERVANT. Hey!

JUST. What is it?

SERVANT. Can you show me the officer who was living in this room until yesterday? (*Pointing to the side from which he has just come.*)

JUST. Yes, I can. What've you got for him?

SERVANT. What we've always got when we haven't got anything. A greeting. It's come to my mistress's ears as how she turned him out of his room. My mistress knows what's what, and so I'm to beg his pardon.

JUST. All right, beg his pardon, there he is.

SERVANT. What is he? What do you call him?

TELLHEIM. My friend, I have already heard your commission. It is an unnecessary piece of courtesy on the part of your mistress, which I recognize for what it is worth. Please give her my respects . . . What is your mistress's name?

SERVANT. What's her name? Oh, she's called "madam."

TELLHEIM. And her family name?

SERVANT. I've never heard that, and it's not my business to ask. I arrange things so that . . . well, I change masters about every six weeks. As far as I'm concerned, to hell with their names!

JUST. Bravo, mate!

SERVANT. I only started with the mistress a few days ago, in Dresden. I think she's looking for her fiancé here.

TELLHEIM. Enough, my friend. I wanted to know your mistress's name, not her secrets. Go!

SERVANT. Brother, I don't think he'd be much of a master for me!

SCENE TEN

TELLHEIM *and* JUST

TELLHEIM. Just, I want you to arrange to get out of this place. I find myself more sensitive to the courtesy of this strange woman than I am to the ill manners of the landlord. Here, take this ring; it's the one valuable thing I have left and the one which I never thought I'd have to put to this use. Pawn it. Raise four hundred talers on it. The innkeeper's bill can't be more than thirty talers. Pay the landlord and then move my things. Where to?... Wherever you like. The cheaper the inn the better. You can meet me in the café next door. I am leaving now; see that you do it properly.

JUST. Don't you worry about that, major.

TELLHEIM, *returning*. And most important of all, don't forget my pistols, which were hanging behind the bed.

JUST. I won't forget anything. Hm, so the master had this valuable ring, and carried it in his pocket and not on his finger. So, landlord, we're not as poor as we seem to be. I know what! I'll pawn it with the landlord. A pretty little ring. He'll be angry, I know, because we're not going to spend all the money in his place. A pretty little ring, I'll ...

SCENE ELEVEN

PAUL WERNER *and* JUST

JUST. Well, if it isn't Werner! Hello, Werner. Welcome to the big city.

WERNER. Damned village! I can't get used to it again. Cheer up, children, cheer up! I am bringing some more money. Where's the major?

JUST. He must have passed you. He just went downstairs.

WERNER. I came up the backstairs. How is he? I would have been here last week, but ...

JUST. What held you up?

WERNER. Just ... Just, have you heard of Prince Heraclius?

JUST. Heraclius? Not that I know of.

WERNER. Haven't you heard about the great hero in the East?

JUST. Well, I know about three wise men from the East, who run about with a star around New Year's time.

WERNER. Man, I think you must read the paper about as little as you read the Bible. You don't know Prince Heraclius. You don't know about the great man who has conquered Persia and is now going to finish off the Turks. Thank God there's somewhere left in the world where there's a war on! I kept hoping it would break out here again. But they're still sitting round licking their wounds. No, once a soldier, always a soldier. But listen. (*Looking round shyly to make sure no one is listening.*) In confidence, Just, I'm going to Persia to fight a campaign or two against the Turks under the leadership of His Royal Highness, Prince Heraclius.

JUST. You?

WERNER. Me! As sure as I'm standing here. Our ancestors used to fight the Turks, and we would too if only we were honest men and good Christians. I know a campaign against the Turks isn't nearly such fun as one against the French. But then the rewards should be greater in this life and the next. Did you know that all Turks' swords are encrusted with diamonds?

JUST. I wouldn't budge a foot to have my head split open by a sword like that. You surely aren't crazy enough to want to leave your farm?

WERNER. I'm taking it with me. Didn't you know? My farm has been sold . . .

JUST. Sold?

WERNER. Sh! . . . Here are the four hundred I got yesterday. They're for the major.

JUST. And what is he supposed to do with them?

WERNER. What d'you think he's supposed to do with them? Eat 'em up, gamble 'em away, drink 'em up . . . well . . . I don't know; he can do what he likes with them. The man's got to have some money, and it's bad enough for him having all this trouble to get his

own. I know what I'd do if I was in your place. I'd
think, "To hell with the lot of them! I'll go with Paul
Werner to Persia." Hell! Prince Heraclius must have
heard of Major Tellheim, too, even if he doesn't know
his old sergeant major, Paul Werner. That business at
Katzenberg . . .

JUST. Shall I tell you about it?

WERNER. *You* tell *me*? . . . I can tell that a good battle
plan is something you don't appreciate. I'm not going
to throw my pearls before swine. Take the four
hundred talers and give them to the major. Tell him
to keep them for me. I've got to go to the market now.
I've brought forty bushels of rye with me, and he can
have that too.

JUST. Werner, I know you mean well, but we don't
want your money. Keep your talers, and you can have
the other five hundred back as soon as you like; we've
not touched them.

WERNER. Really? The major's still got some money, has
he?

JUST. No, he hasn't.

WERNER. Well, has he borrowed some then?

JUST. No.

WERNER. What are you living on then?

JUST. Credit, and when we can't get any more credit and
they throw us out, we shall pawn what we've still got
left and clear out. Listen, Paul, we've got to get even
with this landlord here.

WERNER. If he's done something to the major, I'm with
you.

JUST. What about waiting for him when he comes out
of the tobacconist's this evening and giving him a
going over?

WERNER. This evening? Wait for him? Two against
one? No, that's not right.

JUST. Suppose we burn down his house about his ears?

WERNER. Burn it down? You know, it's easy to tell you were with the baggage train and not in the infantry . . . Pah!

JUST. Supposing we seduced his daughter? Though it's true she's ugly.

WERNER. She'll stay ugly for a long time. Anyway, you don't need my help for that. But what's the matter, what's up?

JUST. Come on and I'll tell you something that'll surprise you.

WERNER. There's the devil to pay round here.

JUST. Come on!

WERNER. So much the better! To Persia! To Persia!

ACT TWO

SCENE ONE

The Lady's Boudoir

MINNA VON BARNHELM *and* FRANZISKA, *her maid*

MINNA, *in her negligée and looking at her watch.* Franziska, we got up very early, we are going to be bored.

FRANZISKA. Well, I don't know who can get any sleep in these big cities, what with the coaches, night watchmen, drums, cats, corporals . . . no end of rattling, shouting, swearing, meowing, just as if the night were made for anything but peace. Would you like a cup of tea, madam?

MINNA. No, I don't feel like tea.

FRANZISKA. I'll get them to make some of our chocolate.

MINNA. Yes do, for yourself.

FRANZISKA. Just for myself? I'd just as soon talk to myself as drink alone . . . Well, it's going to be a long day . . . Out of sheer boredom we shall have to make our toilet and then choose the dress in which we are going to make our first assault.

MINNA. Why do you talk about assaults? You know that I have only come here to demand a surrender.

FRANZISKA. And that officer we turned out, the one we sent our apologies to—he doesn't seem to have the best of manners, otherwise he would at least have asked for the honor of being allowed to pay his respects to us.

MINNA. Not all officers are Tellheims. To tell you the truth, I only sent him my apologies so that I could have the chance to ask him about Tellheim . . . Franziska, my heart tells me that our journey will be successful and that I shall find him.

FRANZISKA. Your heart, madam? I shouldn't put too much trust in your heart. The heart likes to tell us what we want to hear. If our mouths were as ready to say what our hearts wanted them to, we'd have got into the fashion of wearing locks on our mouths long ago.

MINNA. Ha! Ha! You and your locks and mouths! That's a fashion I'd approve of.

FRANZISKA. It's better to keep even the prettiest teeth hidden than to have your heart leaping out over them every few minutes.

MINNA. Really, are you so reserved?

FRANZISKA. No, madam, but I wish I was. People talk very seldom about the virtues they have, but all the more frequently about the ones they don't have.

MINNA. You know, Franziska, that's a very good observation you've made.

FRANZISKA. That I made? Do you really *make* something that just occurs to you?

MINNA. And do you know why I think it's such a good observation? Because it has a lot to do with my Tellheim.

FRANZISKA. Do you ever come across anything that doesn't have some connection with him?

MINNA. Friends and enemies alike say that he is the bravest man in the world. But did anyone ever hear him talk about bravery? He has the most honest heart in the world, but did anyone ever hear him talk about honesty or nobility?

FRANZISKA. What virtues does he talk about then?

MINNA. He doesn't talk about any, because he lacks none of them.

FRANZISKA. That's just what I wanted to hear.

MINNA. Wait a minute, Franziska, I do remember one thing. He often talks about economy. You know, in strictest confidence, Franziska, I think he's a bit of a spendthrift.

FRANZISKA. There's one other thing, madam. I've often heard him talk about his constancy and his faithfulness to you. Supposing he was a bit of a flirt?

MINNA. You beast! . . . But you are not serious, are you, Franziska?

FRANZISKA. How long is it since he wrote to you?

MINNA. He has only written once since the armistice.

FRANZISKA. Another complaint against peace. Wonderful! Peace is supposed to make good all the evil caused by the war, but it also seems to destroy whatever good the war brought about. Peace ought not to be so obstinate, and anyway, how long have we been at peace? Time really drags when there's so little news. There's not much point in having the mails working again—nobody ever writes, because nobody has anything to write about.

MINNA. "Peace has come," he wrote to me, "And I am approaching the fulfillment of my wishes." But that he should have only written to me once . . .

FRANZISKA. So that we have to hasten to help him to the fulfillment of his wishes. If we come across him, we'll make him pay . . . But supposing he had in the meantime fulfilled his wishes, and we were to find out here . . .

MINNA, *fearful and quickly*. That he was dead?

FRANZISKA. Dead to you, madam, in the arms of another.

MINNA. Oh! You torture me. Just you wait, Franziska, he'll pay you out for that! But go on talking or we shall fall asleep. His regiment was disbanded after the armistice. Who knows what confusion he may have got into with his records and accounts. Who knows whether he may not have been posted to another regiment in some distant province. Who knows what the circumstances are . . . There's a knock.

FRANZISKA. Come in!

SCENE TWO

LANDLORD, MINNA, *and* FRANZISKA

LANDLORD, *his head thrust forward.* May I come in gracious ladies?

FRANZISKA. Oh! The landlord. Please come in.

LANDLORD, *a pen behind his ear, a sheet of paper and writing utensils in his hand.* I come, madam, to wish you a most humble good morning . . . (*to* FRANZISKA) and you too, my dear.

FRANZISKA. What a polite man!

MINNA. We thank you.

FRANZISKA. And wish you a good morning, too.

LANDLORD. May I take the liberty of asking how Your Graces rested on your first night under my miserable roof?

FRANZISKA. Well, the roof isn't all that bad, but the beds could have been better.

LANDLORD. What! Don't tell me that you didn't sleep! Perhaps you were overtired from the journey.

MINNA. Perhaps.

LANDLORD. Of course, of course. For otherwise, otherwise . . . In the meantime, if there is anything which is not completely as it should be for Your Graces's comfort, Your Graces have only to tell me.

FRANZISKA. Very well, sir, very well, and incidentally, we are not stupid and an inn is the last place where you should be stupid. We'll tell you how we should like things arranged.

LANDLORD. And now there's another thing . . . (*He takes the pen from behind his ear.*)

FRANZISKA. Well?

LANDLORD. I am sure that Your Graces are familiar with the regulations which, in their wisdom, our police have made.

MINNA. I'm afraid I am completely unfamiliar with them, sir.

LANDLORD. We landlords are directed not to put up any stranger, no matter what his social class or his sex, for more than twenty-four hours without handing in a report to the proper authority as to his name, his home address, character, the business which brings him here, the proposed duration of his visit, etc., etc.

MINNA. Very well.

LANDLORD. Would Your Graces object, therefore . . . (*He goes to the table and prepares to start writing.*)

MINNA. Gladly, my name is . . .

LANDLORD. One moment, if you please. (*Writing.*) Date: 22d August, *anni currentis*, arrived here at the King of Spain . . . Now, your name, madam?

MINNA. Fräulein von Barnhelm.

LANDLORD, *writing*. "Von Barnhelm" . . . and you come from where, madam?

MINNA. From my estates in Saxony.

LANDLORD, *writes*. "Estates in Saxony" . . . Saxony! Ha! Ha! Saxony, madam, Saxony?

FRANZISKA. Well, and why not? I take it it isn't a sin around here to come from Saxony?

LANDLORD. A sin? Oh, heaven forbid! That would be a brand-new sin! So you come from Saxony? Saxony, dear òld Saxony. Well, if I'm right, Saxony isn't exactly what you would call small, and it has several . . . what should I say . . . districts, provinces . . . our police are very precise, madam.

MINNA. I understand; from my estates in Thuringia.

LANDLORD. From Thuringia. Well now, that's better, madam, that's much more precise . . . (*Writes and then reads aloud.*) "Fräulein von Barnhelm coming from her estates in Thuringia together with a lady-in-waiting and two servants."

FRANZISKA. A lady-in-waiting, is that me?

LANDLORD. That's right, my dear.

FRANZISKA. Now, sir, I think you'd better change that to lady's *maid*. I understand that the police here are very precise; there might be a misunderstanding, which could cause me trouble when my banns are read. For I really am still a maid, and my name is Franziska, surname Willing; my father used to be a miller on one of the lady's estates. The village was called Klein-Rammsdorf. My brother owns the mill now. I went to court when I was still very young and was brought up with madam, here. We are the same age, twenty-one next Candlemas. Madam and I learned exactly the same things. It is very important that the police should know exactly who I am.

LANDLORD. Very well, my child, I'll make a note of it in case anyone should enquire. But now, madam, what is your business here?

MINNA. My business?

LANDLORD. Is Your Grace perhaps seeking something from His Majesty, the King?

MINNA. Oh, no!

LANDLORD. Or from the High Court of Justice?

MINNA. No, not that either.

LANDLORD. Or? . . .

MINNA. No, no. I'm just here to look after my own affairs.

LANDLORD. Very well, madam, but what are they?

MINNA. They are . . . Franziska, do you know, I think we're being cross-examined.

FRANZISKA. Sir, surely the police would never insist on knowing a young lady's secrets?

LANDLORD. Oh certainly, my dear, the police want to know everything, absolutely everything, and especially secrets.

FRANZISKA. What shall we do, madam? Listen, sir . . . but it must stay between us and the police.

MINNA, *aside.* Whatever is the idiot going to tell him now?

FRANZISKA. We've come to steal an officer from the king.

LANDLORD. What's that, my dear?

FRANZISKA. Or to let ourselves be stolen by an officer.

MINNA. Franziska, are you mad? Sir, this saucy girl is pulling your leg.

LANDLORD. Well, I hope not. I mean, as far as my humble person is concerned, she can joke with me as much as she likes, but when it comes to our police authorities . . .

MINNA. Do you know what, sir? I really don't know what to do about all this. I should have thought that you might have left all this form-filling business until my uncle arrives. I told you yesterday why he couldn't come with me right away. He had an accident with his coach a couple of miles from here and was determined that the accident shouldn't cause me another night's delay, so I came on ahead. At the very most he'll only be a day later than I.

LANDLORD. All right then, madam, we'll wait for him.

MINNA. He will be able to answer your questions better than I. He knows who he has to tell things to, how much to tell, and what he can keep quiet about.

LANDLORD. So much the better. It's true, you can't ask a young woman (*he looks meaningfully at* FRANZISKA) to treat a serious matter seriously among serious people.

MINNA. And the rooms for my uncle, are they ready?

LANDLORD. Absolutely, madam, absolutely, except for one . . .

FRANZISKA. From which you have had to turn out another honest man?

LANDLORD. It seems, madam, that the lady's maids who come from Saxony are a very sympathetic lot.

MINNA. That's right, sir. What you did was not right. It would have been better for you not to have taken us in at all.

LANDLORD. What do you mean, madam, what do you mean?

MINNA. I hear that the officer who was turned out on our behalf . . .

LANDLORD. Was only a discharged officer, madam.

MINNA. Even so!

LANDLORD. Who's on his last legs.

MINNA. So much the worse. He seems to be a very deserving man . . .

LANDLORD. But I tell you, he is discharged.

MINNA. But the king cannot possibly know every deserving man in his service.

LANDLORD. Oh, yes he does, he knows them, all of them.

MINNA. But he can't reward them all.

LANDLORD. They'd all be rewarded if they'd lived properly. But as long as the war was on, these gentlemen lived as if it was going to last forever, as if the idea of "mine" and "yours" had been abandoned for good. And so now all the inns are full of them, and a landlord has to be pretty careful of them. I've managed to get on pretty well with this one. If he didn't actually have any money left, he had the equivalent. And he could easily have stayed on for another two or three months. Still, it's all for the best. By the way, madam, do you know anything about jewels?

MINNA. Not especially.

LANDLORD. I'm sure Your Grace does. I must show you

a ring, a valuable ring. You know, you have a very beautiful one on your own finger, and I must say that I'm surprised, because the more I look at it the more it looks like the one I have myself. Look, look! (*He takes the ring out of its case.*) Look at that fire, the center diamond alone weighs more than five carats!

MINNA, *looking at the ring*. Where am I? What do I see? This ring . . .

LANDLORD. At a fair estimate it is worth 1500 talers.

MINNA. Franziska, have a look! . . .

LANDLORD. I didn't hesitate for a moment to offer him four hundred for it.

MINNA. Don't you recognize it, Franziska?

FRANZISKA. It's the very same! Sir, where did you get this ring?

LANDLORD. Surely you're not claiming it, my dear?

FRANZISKA. Not claim it? Madam's name is engraved on the inside of it. Show him, madam.

MINNA. This is it! This is it! How did you come by this ring, landlord?

LANDLORD. Me? In the most honorable fashion in the world. Madam, you surely don't want to cause me disgrace and misfortune? How should I know where the ring actually came from? I do know that during the war a lot of things changed hands very often, with or without the knowledge of the rightful owner. War's war, after all. More than one thing has come over the border from Saxony. Give it back to me, madam, please give it back!

MINNA. First tell us who you got it from.

LANDLORD. From a man who I should never have thought such a thing of. From a man, otherwise a very good man ...

MINNA. From the best man under the sun, if you got it from its rightful owner. Hurry, bring this man to me!

He must be the man himself, or at least must know where he is.

LANDLORD. Who, who, madam?

FRANZISKA. Are you deaf? Our major.

LANDLORD. Major, that's right, he is a major, the man who had this room before you, and it's him I got it from.

MINNA. Major von Tellheim?

LANDLORD. Von Tellheim, yes! Do you know him?

MINNA. Do I know him! He was here? Tellheim here? Living in this room? And it was he who pawned the ring with you? How did he get into such an embarrassing situation? Where is he? Does he owe you money? Franziska, bring me the strongbox. Open it! (FRANZISKA *places the box on the table and opens it.*) How much does he owe you? Who else does he owe money to? Bring all his creditors to me here. Here's cash, paper money. Everything belongs to him!

LANDLORD. What's all this?

MINNA. Where is he, where is he?

LANDLORD. He was still here an hour ago.

MINNA. You horrible man, how could you be so unkind to him, so harsh, so cruel?

LANDLORD. Your Grace will forgive me?

MINNA. Hurry, bring him here to me.

LANDLORD. His servant may still be here. Would Your Grace wish me to look for him?

MINNA. Would I? Hurry, run! If you do me this service, I'll overlook your bad treatment of him.

FRANZISKA. Hurry, sir, hurry, hurry, hurry! (*Pushes him out.*)

SCENE THREE

MINNA *and* FRANZISKA

MINNA. I've got him back, Franziska! You see, now I've got him back! I don't know where I am, for sheer joy.

Rejoice with me, dear Franziska. But why should you? But you must, you must rejoice with me. Come, Franziska, I'll give you gifts so that you will rejoice with me. Say something, Franziska, what shall I give you? What would you like best of all the things I have here? Take whatever you like, but rejoice with me. I can see you won't take anything. Wait a minute! (*She looks in the strongbox.*) There you are, dear Franziska (*she gives her money*), buy yourself something you'd like. Ask me for more if that's not enough. But rejoice with me! Oh, it's so sad to have to rejoice alone! Come, take it! . . .

FRANZISKA. I'd be stealing it from you, madam; you're drunk with happiness, drunk.

MINNA. Now, Franziska, I may be a little tipsy, but take it . . . (*She forces her to take the money, pressing it into her hand.*) And don't thank me! Wait a minute, it's a good thing I thought of it. (*She puts her hand into the strongbox again and takes out some more money.*) And this, dear Franziska, set this aside for the first poor wounded soldier who speaks to us.

SCENE FOUR

LANDLORD, MINNA, *and* FRANZISKA

MINNA. Well, is he coming?

LANDLORD. What a miserable, rude fellow he is!

MINNA. Who?

LANDLORD. His servant. He refuses to go and fetch him.

FRANZISKA. Bring the wretch in here. I know all of the major's servants. Which of them was it?

MINNA. Bring him here, quickly. When he sees us, he'll go. (*Exit* LANDLORD.)

SCENE FIVE

MINNA *and* FRANZISKA

MINNA. I can hardly wait. But Franziska, why are you still so cold? Don't you want to rejoice with me?

FRANZISKA. I would like to, from the bottom of my heart, if only . . .

MINNA. If only?

FRANZISKA. We have found the man again, but how have we found him? From all that we hear, things are not going very well with him. He must be unhappy, and that makes me feel sad.

MINNA. Makes you feel sad? Let me hug you for those words, my dearest friend! I will never forget what you said. I am merely in love, but you are really good.

SCENE SIX

LANDLORD, JUST, MINNA, *and* FRANZISKA

LANDLORD. I managed to bring him, but it wasn't easy.

FRANZISKA. A stranger, I don't know him.

MINNA. My friend, you are in the service of Major von Tellheim?

JUST. Yes.

MINNA. Where is your master?

JUST. Not here.

MINNA. But you know where to find him?

JUST. Yes.

MINNA. Will you bring him here quickly?

JUST. No.

MINNA. You would be doing me a favor.

JUST. Ha!

MINNA. And your master a service.

JUST. Maybe, maybe not.

MINNA. What makes you think that?

JUST. Aren't you the strangers that sent their regards to him this morning?

MINNA. Yes.

JUST. I'm right then.

MINNA. Does your master know my name?

JUST. No, but he dislikes over-polite ladies as much as he dislikes over-rude landlords.

LANDLORD. Are you referring to me?

JUST. Yes.

LANDLORD. You don't need to take it out on madam, here. Bring your master here quickly.

MINNA, *to* FRANZISKA. Give him a little something.

FRANZISKA, *trying to press money into* JUST's *hand.* We're not asking you to do this service for nothing.

JUST. And I'm not asking you for money without doing you a service.

FRANZISKA. Fair exchange.

JUST. I can't do it. My master has told me to move his things out. That's what I'm doing, and I'd be grateful if you didn't hold me up any longer. When I'm finished, I'll tell him that he can come here. He's next door in the cafe, and when he can't find anything better to do there, he'll probably come up here. (*Starts to leave.*)

FRANZISKA. Wait a moment . . . Madam is the major's . . . sister.

MINNA. Yes, yes, his sister.

JUST. I know better than that. The major hasn't got any sisters. Twice in six months, he sent me to his family in the Kurland. Of course, there are all kinds of sisters.

FRANZISKA. You scoundrel!

JUST. Don't you have to be a scoundrel if you're going to get people to let you go? (*Exit.*)

FRANZISKA. Devil!

LANDLORD. Well, I told you. Let him go. I know now where his master is. I'll fetch him myself at once. But, madam, I ask you most humbly to make excuses to the major, for my having had the misfortune to have to turn away, against my will, a man of his worth.

MINNA. Go quickly landlord. I will see that everything is all right. (*Exit* LANDLORD.) Franziska, run after him, quickly, he must not mention my name. (*Exit* FRANZISKA.)

SCENE SEVEN

MINNA *and, afterwards,* FRANZISKA

MINNA. I have him again! . . . Am I alone? I don't want to be alone for nothing. (*She folds her hands.*) I am not alone! (*Looking up.*) One single, thankful thought directed to heaven is the most perfect prayer. I have found him, I have found him! (*She flings her arms wide.*) I am happy, what can be more pleasing to God's eyes than a joyful creature. (*Enter* FRANZISKA.) Back again, Franziska? . . . You feel sorry for him. I don't feel sorry for him. I am not sorry for him. Unhappiness is good, too. Perhaps heaven took everything away from him just so that I could give him everything back in the shape of myself.

FRANZISKA. He may be here any moment, and you are still in your negligée, madam. Why don't you get dressed quickly?

MINNA. Go, please. From now on he will see me like this more often than he will see me in full toilette.

FRANZISKA. You certainly know what suits you best, madam.

MINNA. Right again.

FRANZISKA. A beautiful woman is most beautiful without makeup.

MINNA. Do we have to be beautiful? I suppose it's necessary for us to think that we are beautiful. As long as he thinks I'm beautiful . . . Franziska, if all young girls feel as I do at this moment, we are . . . Strange feelings! Tender and proud, virtuous yet vain, voluptuous and pious . . . You can't understand me, I don't think that I understand myself. Joy makes you dizzy, giddy.

FRANZISKA. Please, pull yourself together, madam, I hear someone coming.

MINNA. Pull myself together? Shall I receive him without showing him my feelings?

SCENE EIGHT

TELLHEIM, LANDLORD, MINNA, *and* FRANZISKA

TELLHEIM, *seeing* MINNA *and at once rushing up to her.* Minna!

MINNA, *going toward him.* Tellheim!

TELLHEIM, *stopping suddenly and turning back.* Forgive me, madam . . . but to find Fräulein von Barnhelm here . . .

MINNA. Surely it can't be entirely unexpected? (*As she moves nearer to him, he withdraws further.*) Am I to forgive you because I am still your Minna? Heaven forgive you that I am still Fräulein von Barnhelm!

TELLHEIM. Madam . . . (*He looks at the* LANDLORD *and shrugs his shoulders.*)

MINNA, *growing aware of the* LANDLORD *waves to* FRANZISKA. My good man . . .

TELLHEIM. If we are not both mistaken . . .

FRANZISKA. Sir, who's this you've brought us? Come along, quickly, let's go and find the right one.

LANDLORD. Isn't he the right one? He must be!

FRANZISKA. Oh no, he mustn't. Hurry up, I haven't said good morning to your daughter yet.

LANDLORD, *without budging*. Oh, a great honor, I'm sure . . .

FRANZISKA, *taking hold of him*. Come, we have to look at the menu. Let's see what we're going to have . . .

LANDLORD. The first thing you're going to have . . .

FRANZISKA. Quiet, quiet, if madam knows beforehand what she's going to have for lunch, it spoils her appetite. Come, you must tell me on my own what we are going to have. (*Forces him to go.*)

SCENE NINE

TELLHEIM *and* MINNA

MINNA. Are we still making a mistake?

TELLHEIM. I wish to heaven we were! But there is only one Minna, and you are she.

MINNA. What a lot of fuss! Why shouldn't the whole world hear what we have to say to one another.

TELLHEIM. You here? What are you doing here, madam?

MINNA. I have done what I wanted to. (*Runs to him with open arms.*) I have found everything that I was looking for.

TELLHEIM, *backing away*. You were looking for a happy man, worthy of your love, and you find . . . a wretched one.

MINNA. So you love me no longer; you love someone else.

TELLHEIM. A man who could love someone else could never have loved you.

MINNA. You remove but one sting from my heart. If I have lost your love, what difference does it make whether it is indifference or another woman's charms which have taken you from me. You no longer love me, and yet you do not love another. Unhappy man, if you have no one to love!

TELLHEIM. True, madam. He who is unhappy must not love anyone or anything at all. He deserves his misfortune if he does not know how to gain this victory over himself, if he can permit himself to stand by and allow those whom he loves to participate in his misfortune. Ever since reason and necessity have bidden me to forget Minna von Barnhelm, what an effort I have made! I had just begun to hope that this effort would not forever be in vain . . . and you appear, madam.

MINNA. Do I understand you correctly? One moment, sir, let us see where we are before we say anything more. Would you answer me just one question?

TELLHEIM. As many as you like, madam.

MINNA. Will you answer me without quibbling or evading the issue? With nothing but a simple "yes" or "no"?

TELLHEIM. I will if I can.

MINNA. You can. Good! Forget for the moment the effort which you made to forget me . . . Do you still love me, Tellheim?

TELLHEIM. Madam, this question . . .

MINNA. You promised to answer only "yes" or "no."

TELLHEIM. But I did add, "If I can."

MINNA. You can. You must know what is happening in your own heart. Do you still love me, Tellheim, yes or no?

TELLHEIM. If my heart . . .

MINNA. Yes or no?

TELLHEIM. Well, yes.

MINNA. Yes?

TELLHEIM. Yes, yes, except . . .

MINNA. Patience! . . . You still love me, that is enough for me . . . What kind of tone am I using? A hostile,

melancholic, infectious one. I shall use my own again.
Now, my beloved, unhappy one. You still love me and
you still have your Minna, why are you unhappy?
Let me tell you what a vain and foolish creature
your Minna was . . . still is. She allowed herself,
allows herself, to dream that she was your whole
happiness. Quickly, show her the cause of your
unhappiness and let her see how much of it she can
counterbalance. Well?

TELLHEIM. Madam, I am not in the habit of complaining.

MINNA. Very well. I certainly cannot imagine a quality,
after boastfulness, which would please me less in a
soldier than complaining. But there is a certain cold,
disinterested way in which we can speak about misfortune and bravery.

TELLHEIM. Which is still boasting and complaining
nevertheless.

MINNA. Argue, argue, argue! In that case you should
never have called yourself unhappy. Either you should
keep quiet about the whole business or else bring it all
out into the open. So reason and necessity bid you
forget me? I am a great admirer of reason, and I have
a great deal of respect for necessity; but tell me, at
least, how reasonable this reason is, how necessary this
necessity.

TELLHEIM. Very well, then, madam, listen. You call me
Tellheim, and that is indeed my name. But you
imagine at the same time that I am the same Tellheim
you knew in your native country, a man in the bloom
of youth, full of prospects, full of ambition, a man
completely in control of his body and his soul, to
whom every frontier of honor and happiness was open,
who was worthy of your hand and your heart, and even
if he was not worthy of you yourself, hoped daily to
grow more worthy. I am as far from being this
Tellheim as I am from being my own father. Both

belong to the past. I am Tellheim, the discharged
soldier, with his honor wounded, Tellheim the cripple
and the beggar. You promised yourself to the other
Tellheim; do you wish to keep your word to this one?

MINNA. That sounds very tragic . . . but, sir, until I find
the other one again—for after all, I am really rather
fond of Tellheims—this one will do for the moment.
Give me your hand, dear beggar. (*Takes his hand.*)

TELLHEIM, *putting his other hand in front of his face and
turning away from her.* This is too much! . . . Where
am I? Let me go, madam! Your goodness tortures
me! Let me go!

MINNA. What has come over you? Where do you want to
go?

TELLHEIM. Away from you!

MINNA. Away from me? (*Draws his hand to her breast.*)
Dreamer!

TELLHEIM. My dear, desperation will throw me, at
your feet.

MINNA. Away from me?

TELLHEIM. Yes, away from you, never, never to see you
again, or at least I am so firmly resolved, so absolutely
resolved to do nothing contemptible—nor to allow
you to do anything thoughtless. Let me go, Minna!
(*Breaks away, exit.*)

MINNA, *calling after him.* Minna let you go? Tellheim!
Tellheim!

ACT THREE

SCENE ONE

The Parlor

JUST, *a letter in his hand.* Have I got to come back into this damned house again? A note from my master to the young lady who says she's his sister. I hope there's nothing brewing there. Otherwise there'll be no end of carrying notes backward and forward. I'll be glad to get rid of this note, but I don't want to have to go up to the room. The women ask such a lot of questions, and I don't like answering them. Wait a minute, the door's opening. How lucky! It's the lady's maid.

SCENE TWO

FRANZISKA *and* JUST

FRANZISKA, *calling back through the door through which she has just come.* Don't worry, I'll take care. (*She catches sight of Just.*) Look out, here's something got in my way already; but there's nothing I can do with this brute.

JUST. Your servant . . .

FRANZISKA. I wouldn't want a servant like that.

JUST. Oh well, it's only a manner of speaking. I was just bringing a note from my master to your mistress, the young lady . . . his sister . . . wasn't that it? Sister?

FRANZISKA. Give it to me! (*Snatches the note from his hand.*)

JUST. "Will you be good enough," my master says, "to give it to her? And afterwards would you be good enough," my master says . . . I don't want you to think that *I* am asking for anything.

FRANZISKA. Well?

JUST. My master knows what's what. He knows that the way to a young lady is through her maid . . . at least, I imagine so. Would the young maid be so good, my master says, and let him know whether he might have the pleasure of speaking to the young maid for a quarter of an hour.

FRANZISKA. Do you mean me?

JUST. You'll excuse me if I'm giving you a title which you no longer have any right to . . . Yes, you . . . Just a quarter of an hour, but alone, absolutely alone, tête-à-tête. He has something very important to tell you.

FRANZISKA. Well, I've got a few things to tell him. He can come if he wants to. I'll wait for him.

JUST. But when can he come? When is most convenient? This evening?

FRANZISKA. What do you mean? Your master can come when he wants to, and now be off with you.

JUST. With pleasure. (*Starts to leave.*)

FRANZISKA. Wait a minute, there's just one more thing. Where are the major's other servants?

JUST. The other ones? They're . . . here, there, and everywhere.

FRANZISKA. Where's William?

JUST. The valet? The major sent him off on a trip.

FRANZISKA. Oh? And Philip, where is he?

JUST. The gamekeeper? The major left him in good hands.

FRANZISKA. Doubtless because there's no hunting at the moment. But what about Martin?

JUST. The coachman? He went out for a ride.

FRANZISKA. And Fritz?

JUST. The footman? He's been given a promotion.

FRANZISKA. Where were you, then, when the major was with us in Thuringia in his winter quarters? You weren't with him at that time.

JUST. Oh yes, I was a groom, but I was in the hospital at the time.

FRANZISKA. A groom? But what are you now?

JUST. A bit of everything—valet, gamekeeper, footman, and groom.

FRANZISKA. Well I declare! Letting so many good people go and keeping the worst one of all. I'd like to know what your master sees in you.

JUST. Perhaps he thinks I'm an honest man.

FRANZISKA. People who are just honest don't amount to much. William was a different sort of chap . . . and your master's let him go off on a trip?

JUST. Yes, he's let him . . . he can't stop him.

FRANZISKA. What do you mean?

JUST. William'll cut a good figure on his travels; he took the master's whole wardrobe with him.

FRANZISKA. What? Do you mean he made off with it?

JUST. Well, you couldn't exactly say that, but after we left Nuremberg, he didn't bother to follow us with it.

FRANZISKA. What a rogue!

JUST. He was quite a chap—could cut your hair, shave you, chat with you . . . and charm you . . . couldn't he?

FRANZISKA. But still! I wouldn't have let the gamekeeper go if I'd been the major. Even if he couldn't use him as a gamekeeper, he was a hard-working sort of a chap. . . . Who's looking after him now?

JUST. The Commandant of Spandau.

FRANZISKA. The fort? There surely isn't much hunting on the ramparts, is there?

JUST. Well, Philip isn't actually hunting there, either.

FRANZISKA. What's he doing then?

JUST. He's pushing a wheelbarrow.

FRANZISKA. Pushing a wheelbarrow?

JUST. Only for three years. He hatched a little plot among the soldiers in my master's company and wanted to take six deserters through the lines.

FRANZISKA. I can't believe it! The devil!

JUST. Oh! He's a hard-working chap all right; he knows all the highways and byways for fifty miles round, and he can shoot, too.

FRANZISKA. It's lucky the major still has his good old coachman.

JUST. Has he still got him?

FRANZISKA. I thought you said that Martin was out somewhere, so I suppose he'll be back?

JUST. Do you think so?

FRANZISKA. Where's he gone to?

JUST. It's about ten weeks since he rode off with the master's one and only horse.

FRANZISKA. And the rogue hasn't come back yet?

JUST. Of course he may have taken a drop more to drink than his horse. . . . He was a proper coachman, he was! He'd driven in Vienna for ten years. The master won't get another like him. Why, when the horses were at full gallop, he only had to say "Whoa," and they stood stockstill. And what's more, he was a trained horse-doctor.

FRANZISKA. After all that, I feel a bit worried about the footman's promotion.

JUST. No, no, that worked out all right. He's a drummer in a garrison regiment.

FRANZISKA. I thought he'd be all right.

JUST. Fritz got in with a bad lot, never came home at night, ran up debts everywhere in the master's name, and got into a thousand dirty bits of business. In

short, the major saw that he really wanted to rise in
the world (*he pantomimes hanging*), so he helped him
along the way.

FRANZISKA. Wretch!

JUST. But he's a perfect footman. Give him a fifty-pace
start, and my master couldn't overtake him with his
fastest horse. But I wouldn't mind betting that Fritz
could give the gallows a thousand-pace start and he'd
still catch up with it. They were all close friends of
yours, were they? William, Philip, Martin, and Fritz?
Well, Just, the last of 'em, bids you good day.

SCENE THREE

FRANZISKA *and, afterwards, the* LANDLORD

FRANZISKA, *looking earnestly after him.* I deserved that.
Thank you, Just. I set too low a price on honesty. I
won't forget the lesson you've taught me. Oh, what
an unlucky man! (*Turns and is about to go into*
MINNA'*s room when the* LANDLORD *enters.*)

LANDLORD. Wait a minute, my dear.

FRANZISKA. I don't have time at the moment.

LANDLORD. Just one little moment . . . Still no more
news of the major? Surely he hasn't left?

FRANZISKA. What else?

LANDLORD. Didn't your mistress tell you? When I left
you down in the kitchen, my dear, I happened to
come back into this room.

FRANZISKA. You just happened to, so that you could do a
bit of eavesdropping.

LANDLORD. My dear child, how could you think such a
thing of me? There's nothing worse than an inquisitive
landlord. I hadn't been here long when the door of
madam's room suddenly burst open. The major rushed
out, the young lady following him, both in such a

hurry and looking like . . . you can't describe it. She grabbed hold of him, he tore himself away, she grabbed him again. "Tellheim!" "Madam, let me go!" "Where are you going?" He dragged her to the head of the stairs like this, and I was afraid they were going to fall down, but he slipped out of her clutches. The young lady stood there wringing her hands. Then she suddenly turned round, ran to the window, from the window back to the stairs; from the stairs she turned to pacing up and down in this room. I was standing there, and she passed me three times without seeing me. Then she seemed to see me but—and God save us! —I think the young lady thought I was you, my dear. "Franziska," she cried, looking at me. "Am I happy now?" I looked straight up at the ceiling. And again, "Am I happy now?" Honestly, I didn't know what to do till she ran to her door. Then she turned to me again and said, "Come along, Franziska," and went in.

FRANZISKA. You must have dreamt it.

LANDLORD. Dreamt it? No, my child, you don't dream as clearly as that. Yes, I'd give a lot . . . not that I'm nosey mind . . . but I'd give a lot to have the key to that.

FRANZISKA. The key? To our door? That's on the inside, sir. We took it in last night; we're scared.

LANDLORD. I don't mean a key like that. What I mean, my dear, is a key, like an explanation, of everything I saw.

FRANZISKA. Ah, yes! . . . Adieu, sir. Are we going to eat soon?

LANDLORD. Don't forget, my dear, what I really wanted to say.

FRANZISKA. Well? But make it quick!

LANDLORD. The young lady still has my ring; I call it mine . . .

FRANZISKA. It's in good hands, I can assure you.

LANDLORD. I'm not worried about that. I just wanted to remind you. You see, I don't even want it back again. I can easily guess how she knew the ring and why it looked so like her own. She's the best one to look after it. I don't want it any more, and I'll charge the young lady's account with the five hundred talers I lent on it. That's all right, my dear, isn't it?

SCENE FOUR

PAUL WERNER, LANDLORD, *and* FRANZISKA

WERNER. There he is!

FRANZISKA. Five hundred talers? I thought it was only four hundred.

LANDLORD. That's right, four hundred and fifty, only four hundred and fifty, all right my dear, that's what I'll do.

FRANZISKA. All right, we'll see.

WERNER, *coming up behind her and then clapping her on the shoulder*. Little lady, little lady!

FRANZISKA, *alarmed*. Hey!

WERNER. Don't be frightened, little lady. You're pretty and a stranger here, and pretty strangers have to be warned. Little lady, beware of this man. (*Points at* LANDLORD.)

LANDLORD. What an unexpected pleasure! Herr Paul Werner! Welcome to my house, welcome. Still the same old jolly, comical, honest Paul Werner . . . You beware of me, my dear. Ha! Ha! Ha!

WERNER. Keep out of his way.

LANDLORD. Out of my way? Am I a danger? Ha! Ha! Ha! It gets better and better, doesn't it, my dear? He knows how to joke. Me, a danger? Me? Now twenty years ago there might have been something in it. Yes, my dear, then I was a danger, but now . . .

WERNER. There's no fool like an old fool.

LANDLORD. That's the trouble. When we get old, we're not a danger any longer. You'll be in the same boat, one day, Herr Werner!

WERNER. I've never heard anything like it! Young lady, you know that I wasn't talking about that sort of danger. One devil was cast out, and seven others have taken its place.

LANDLORD. Listen to him, just listen to him! See how he's managed to bring the subject round agan! One, joke after another, and always something niew. Oh he's a splendid man, is our Paul Werner! (*Whispering to* FRANZISKA) And a wealthy man, too, and a bachelor. He has a farm about three miles away. He made a little pile in the war . . . and was a sergeant major in the major's regiment. Oh, yes, he's a real friend, one who would die for him.

WERNER. Yes, and you're a friend of my major's . . . one he ought to have killed.

LANDLORD. What! No, Herr Werner, that's not a nice joke at all. Me not a friend of the major's? . . . No, that's a joke I can't understand.

WERNER. Just told me a few nice things about you.

LANDLORD. Just? I thought I recognized the voice of Just in this. Just is an evil-speaking, mean fellow. Now here's a nice young thing who can tell you whether I'm a friend of the major's or not, whether I haven't done him a few services. And why shouldn't I be a friend of the major's? Isn't he a worthy man? It's true he had the misfortune to be discharged, but what does that matter? The king can't know all the worthy men under his command, and if he did know them, he can't reward all of them.

WERNER. Lucky for you that you said that! But Just . . . there's certainly nothing special about Just, but he isn't a liar. And if what he told me was true . . .

LANDLORD. I don't want to hear anything about Just. As I said, this pretty child here can speak.—(*whispering*) You know, my dear, the ring.—Tell Herr Werner. That way he'll get to know me better. And so that it won't appear as if you're just talking to please me, I'll leave you. But you'll have to repeat it to me, Herr Werner, repeat it and tell me whether Just isn't a filthy slanderer.

SCENE FIVE

PAUL WERNER *and* FRANZISKA

WERNER. Well, little lady, so you know my major?

FRANZISKA. Major von Tellheim? Certainly I know him; he's a good man.

WERNER. Isn't he a good man? Are you perhaps a friend of his?

FRANZISKA. From the bottom of my heart.

WERNER. Really? You know, little lady, when you say that, you seem twice as pretty to me. But what are these services that the landlord says he did for the major?

FRANZISKA. I'm sure I don't know, unless he's trying to take credit for something which happened by chance because of his rotten behavior.

WERNER. So it was true, what Just told me? (*Turning to the side where the* LANDLORD *has exited.*) Lucky for you that you left! He really turned him out of his room? Imagine playing a trick like that on a man like that, simply because the idiot thought the major didn't have any money left! The major, no money!

FRANZISKA. What, you mean the major does have money?

WERNER. Piles of it! He doesn't know how much he's got. He doesn't know who owes him what. I owe him money myself, and I'm bringing him a bit here. Look, little lady, here in this purse (*taking a purse from his pocket*) are five hundred talers. And in this little roll (*he takes the roll from his other pocket*), three hundred. All his money.

FRANZISKA. Really? Then why does the major have to pawn things? He pawned a ring . . .

WERNER. Pawned! Don't you believe it! Perhaps he just wanted to get rid of the rubbish.

FRANZISKA. But it's not rubbish! It's a valuable ring which he received from a very dear person.

WERNER. That's it then. From a very dear person. A thing like that often reminds you of something you'd rather not be reminded of. So you get rid of it.

FRANZISKA. What?

WERNER. Some funny things happen to a soldier when he's in winter quarters. There's nothing to do, so out of boredom and to amuse himself, he strikes up acquaintances which he intends only for the winter, but which the kind hearts with whom he forms them assume are for life; and the next thing you know, someone's popped a ring on his finger. He doesn't know how it got there. And as often as not, he'd gladly cut off his finger to get rid of the ring.

FRANZISKA. Oh! And do you think that happened to the major?

WERNER. I'm sure of it. Especially in Saxony. If he'd had ten fingers on each hand, all twenty of them would have had rings on them.

FRANZISKA, *aside*. This sounds odd. We'll have to look into it. Herr Werner . . .

WERNER. Little lady, if it's all the same to you, I'd rather you called me sergeant major.

FRANZISKA. All right, sergeant major, but I've got a note here from the major to my mistress. I'll just take it in quickly, and I'll be back at once. Will you be good enough to wait? I'd like to stay and chat with you a bit longer.

WERNER. Do you like having a chat, little lady? It's all right with me. Go on. I like a chat, too. I'll wait for you.

FRANZISKA. Yes, please wait! (*Exit.*)

SCENE SIX

WERNER

WERNER. That's not a bad little lady; but I should never have promised to wait, because the most important thing is to find the major. So, he doesn't want my money and would rather pawn things. That's typical, but I've thought of a dodge. When I was in town two weeks ago, I visited Marloff's widow. The poor woman was ill and was lamenting the fact that her dead husband owed the major four hundred talers, and she didn't know how she was going to pay him. I was going to see her again today and tell her that when I get the money for my farm, I could lend her five hundred talers. I wanted some of the money to be safe in case things don't work out in Persia. But she'd left, and I'm certain she hasn't been able to pay the major. Yes, that's what I'll do, and the sooner the better. The little lady mustn't mind, but I can't wait for her at the moment. (*Exits deep in thought and almost collides with* TELLHEIM *who enters at that moment.*)

SCENE SEVEN

TELLHEIM *and* WERNER

TELLHEIM. Lost in thought, Werner?

WERNER. Ah, there you are. I was just coming to call on you in your new quarters, major.

TELLHEIM. So that you could bombard my ears with curses against the landlord of my old ones? Please spare me that.

WERNER. I would probably have done that as well. But what I really wanted to do was to thank you for looking after the five hundred talers for me. Just gave them back to me. I must admit that I would have been grateful if you could have kept them for me a bit longer. But you've moved to new quarters which neither of us knows anything about. Who knows what it's like there. They might be stolen from you, and then you'd have to replace them. There'd be no help for it. And I can't give you that responsibility.

TELLHEIM, *smiling*. How long have you been that careful, Werner?

WERNER. It's something you learn. You can't be too careful with your money these days. And there was another thing, Major, from Frau Marloff. I just came from her. Her husband owed you four hundred talers; here are three hundred as a payment. She'll send you the rest next week. It could be that I'm the cause of her not sending the whole sum, because she owed me a taler and eighty groschen, and as she thought I'd come to dun her for it, she paid me out of the money she'd set aside for you. It's easier for you to wait a few days for your money than it is for me to do without my few groschen. There you are. (*Hands him the roll of money.*)

TELLHEIM. Werner!

WERNER. What are you staring at me like that for? Take it, sir!

TELLHEIM. Werner!

WERNER. What's the matter, what's upset you?

TELLHEIM, *bitterly, striking himself on the forehead and stamping his foot*. That . . . that the whole four hundred talers aren't there.

WERNER. But, major, didn't you understand what I said?

TELLHEIM. It's just because I did understand you! Why is it that today it is the finest people who torment me the most?

WERNER. What did you say?

TELLHEIM. You're only half the trouble . . . Leave me, Werner! (*He pushes aside the hand in which* WERNER *holds the money.*)

WERNER. As soon as I've got rid of this.

TELLHEIM. Werner, supposing I was to tell you that Frau Marloff had been here early this morning?

WERNER. Well?

TELLHEIM. That she doesn't owe me anything?

WERNER. Really?

TELLHEIM. That she paid everything down to the last penny? What would you say to that?

WERNER, *pausing for a moment*. I'd say that I'd lied and that lying is a foul game, because you can get caught.

TELLHEIM. And would you feel ashamed of yourself?

WERNER. But what about the person who forced me into lying, what about him? Shouldn't he be ashamed of himself? Now look, major, if I didn't come straight out and tell you that I don't like the way you're carrying on, I'd be lying again, and I don't want to lie any more.

TELLHEIM. Don't be angry, Werner! I recognize your goodness of heart and your affection for me, but I don't need your money.

WERNER. You don't need it, and you'd rather sell things and pawn things and have people talking about you?

TELLHEIM. I don't care if people know that I have nothing left. No one should wish to appear more wealthy than he is.

WERNER. But why should he appear poorer? As long

as our friends have means, we have means ourselves.

TELLHEIM. It would not be proper for me to be in
your debt.

WERNER. Wouldn't be proper? Don't you remember
that day when the sun and the enemy were warming
things up for us and your groom had got lost with
the canteens and you came to me and said, "Werner,
have you got anything to drink?" and I handed you
my water bottle and you took it and drank? Was that
proper? God bless my soul! If a drink of stagnant
water at that time wasn't worth more than all this
rubbish! (*Taking out the purse and offering that to*
TELLHEIM.) Please take it, major! Imagine it's water.
God made money for everybody, too.

TELLHEIM. You're torturing me. You heard me; I do
not want to be in your debt.

WERNER. First it wasn't proper, and now you don't
want to be. Well that's something different again.
(*Somewhat angrily.*) You don't want to be in my debt,
but supposing you were already in my debt, major?
Or don't you owe anything to the man who warded
off the blow that would have split your head in two,
or who another time chopped off the arm which was
going to shoot you through the heart? How can you
get further into his debt? Or is my neck worth less
than my purse? If that's your way of thinking, then
God bless my soul, it's a pretty poor way.

TELLHEIM. Who are you talking to like this, Werner?
We are alone, and now I can say it. If a third party
were to hear, it would sound like a lot of humbug. I'll
gladly admit that I have you to thank for saving my
life on a couple of occasions. But my friend, wouldn't
I, if the opportunity had arisen, have done exactly
the same for you?

WERNER. If the opportunity had arisen? No one has any

doubts about that. Haven't I seen you risk your life for the commonest of soldiers when he was in a jam?

TELLHEIM. Very well!

WERNER. But . . .

TELLHEIM. Why can't you understand me? I say, it is not proper for me to be in your debt; I do not wish to be in your debt. At least not under the circumstances in which I find myself at the moment.

WERNER. Ah ha! You want to wait till things get better. You want to borrow money from me another time, when you don't need it, when you've got money and I haven't.

TELLHEIM. No one should borrow if they don't know how they're going to pay the money back.

WERNER. But a man like you can't always be in need.

TELLHEIM. You know the world. The last person to borrow money from is someone who needs it himself.

WERNER. Oh! That's me, is it? What do I need it for? If you need a sergeant major, then you pay him.

TELLHEIM. You need it so that you can become more than a mere sergeant major. So that you can make your way in a career in which even the worthiest man cannot succeed if he has no money.

WERNER. Be more than a sergeant major? I wouldn't dream of it. I'm a good sergeant major; I might become a bad captain and certainly a worse general. I've seen plenty of that.

TELLHEIM. Please don't make me think anything which is not worthy of you, Werner. I was not exactly pleased to hear what Just told me. You've sold your farm and want to go off on your travels again. I would rather not have to think that it's not the career that you enjoy, but the wild dissolute life which, regrettably, goes with it. A man should be a soldier in order to fight for his country or for a cause, not to serve here today and there tomorrow. That's no better than being a butcher's boy.

WERNER. Well, you're right major. I follow you. You know better what is right and proper. I'll stay with you . . . But major, please take my money for the time being. Sooner or later your whole business will be settled. You'll get piles of money. Then you can pay me back with interest. I'm only doing it for the interest.

TELLHEIM. Be quiet!

WERNER. God bless my soul! I'm only doing it for the interest. Sometimes when I think, "What's going to happen to you in your old age, when you're hacked to bits, when you're penniless, when you have to go begging?"; then I conclude, "No, you won't have to go begging; you'll go to Major Tellheim; he'll share his last penny with you; he'll look after you on your death bed; he'll see that you die as an honest man."

TELLHEIM, *taking* WERNER's *hand.* And, my friend, don't you still think so?

WERNER. No, I don't think so any more. If someone won't accept something from me when he needs it and I have it, he won't give me anything when he has it and I need it . . . That's all! (*Starts to exit.*)

TELLHEIM. Don't drive me out of my mind! Where are you going? (*Holds him back.*) Suppose I were to assure you, on my honor, that I still have some money, that I will tell you when I haven't got any more, and that you will be the first and only person from whom I will borrow any? Will that satisfy you?

WERNER. It'll have to . . . Give me your hand on it, major!

TELLHEIM. There, Paul! . . . Now, that's enough. I came here to talk to a certain young lady.

SCENE EIGHT

FRANZISKA, *coming out of* MINNA'*s room*, TELLHEIM, *and* WERNER

FRANZISKA, *coming out.* Are you still there, sergeant major? (*She sees* TELLHEIM.) And you're there too, major? I will be with you in an instant. (*Goes quickly back into the room.*)

SCENE NINE

TELLHEIM *and* PAUL WERNER

TELLHEIM. That was her! . . . But it sounds as if you know her, eh Werner?

WERNER. Yes, I know the little lady.

TELLHEIM. And yet if I remember correctly, when I was in winter quarters in Thuringia, you were not with me?

WERNER. No, I was seeing about some pieces of equipment in Leipzig.

TELLHEIM. Then how do you come to know her?

WERNER. Our acquaintanceship is still in its infancy. It dates from today. But a young acquaintanceship is a warm one.

TELLHEIM. Then have you also met her mistress?

WERNER. Is her mistress a young lady? She told me that you knew her mistress.

TELLHEIM. Didn't you hear? From Thuringia.

WERNER. Is the lady young?

TELLHEIM. Yes.

WERNER. Beautiful?

TELLHEIM. Very beautiful.

WERNER. Rich?

TELLHEIM. Very rich.

WERNER. Is the young lady as friendly with you as the girl? That would be splendid.

TELLHEIM. What do you mean?

SCENE TEN

FRANZISKA, *coming out of the room again with a letter in her hand*, TELLHEIM, *and* PAUL WERNER

FRANZISKA. Major . . .

TELLHEIM. My dear Franziska, I haven't had the chance to bid you welcome yet.

FRANZISKA. I'm sure you've already done so in your thoughts. I know that you like me. And I like you, too. But it is not fair to frighten people whom you like.

WERNER, *aside*. Ha! Now I understand! That's right.

TELLHEIM. What is my fate, Franziska? Have you given her the letter?

FRANZISKA. Yes, and this one is for you. (*Hands him the letter.*)

TELLHEIM. An answer?

FRANZISKA. No, your own letter back.

TELLHEIM. What? Would she not read it?

FRANZISKA. She wanted to, but . . . we can't read writing very well.

TELLHEIM. You're teasing me.

FRANZISKA. And we think that letter-writing is not for those who can communicate by word-of-mouth whenever they like to.

TELLHEIM. What an excuse! She must read it. It contains the justification . . . all the reasons and grounds . . .

FRANZISKA. Madam would like to hear them from your own lips and not read about them.

TELLHEIM. To hear them from my own lips? So that her every word, her every expression will confuse me?

So that I shall be able to see in her every glance how great my loss is?

FRANZISKA. She shows no mercy! . . . Take it! (*Gives him the letter.*) She will expect you at three. She wants to drive out and look at the town. You are to go with her.

TELLHEIM. Go with her?

FRANZISKA. And what will you give me if I let you go alone? I am going to stay at home.

TELLHEIM. Alone?

FRANZISKA. In a nice closed carriage.

TELLHEIM. Impossible!

FRANZISKA. Yes, yes. In a carriage you will have to face the music. You can't escape from us in a carriage. That's why we've arranged it like that. In short, major, you will come at three sharp. Well? You wanted to speak to me alone as well. What have you got to say to me? . . . But we are not alone. (*She catches sight of* WERNER.)

TELLHEIM. Oh yes, Franziska, we would be alone, but as your mistress has not read the letter, I have nothing to say to you.

FRANZISKA. Oh? So we would be alone? You have no secrets from the sergeant major?

TELLHEIM. No, none.

FRANZISKA. And yet it seems to me that there are some you should have.

TELLHEIM. What do you mean?

WERNER. Why should he, little lady?

FRANZISKA. Especially secrets of a certain sort . . . all twenty, sergeant major? (*Holding up both hands with the fingers spread apart.*)

WERNER. Sh, Sh, little lady!

TELLHEIM. What's that?

FRANZISKA. "And the next thing you know someone's popped a ring on your finger before you know where you are," eh, sergeant major?

TELLHEIM. What are you two talking about?

WERNER. Little lady, little lady, surely you understand a joke?

TELLHEIM. Werner, surely you haven't forgotten what I have told you so many times? There is a certain point beyond which you should not joke with women.

WERNER. God bless my soul, I may have forgotten . . . Little lady, please . . .

FRANZISKA. Well, if it was a joke, I'll forgive you this time.

TELLHEIM. If I really have to come, Franziska, please see that your mistress reads the letter before I arrive. That will save me some of the pain of having to think things and say things again, which I would so gladly forget. There, give it to her. (*He gives the letter back to her, and in so doing becomes aware that it has been opened.*) Do my eyes deceive me, Franziska, or has this letter been opened?

FRANZISKA. Perhaps it has. (*Looks at it.*) That's right, it has been opened. I wonder who did that. But we really haven't read it, major, really. We don't want to read it, because the writer is coming in person. But please come and . . . do you know what, major? Don't come as you are now, in boots, with your hair scarcely combed. Of course we excuse you; you hadn't expected us. Come in shoes, and have your hair combed. This way you look much too virtuous, much too Prussian!

TELLHEIM. Thank you, Franziska.

FRANZISKA. You look as if you'd camped out last night.

TELLHEIM. You may not be so far wrong.

FRANZISKA. We are going to get ready right away too, and then èat. We would be happy to invite you to join us, but we fear that your presence might hinder our eating; and we are not so much in love that our appetites have been spoiled.

TELLHEIM. I'm going. Franziska, please prepare her a
little so that I shall not grow despicable in her eyes or
my own. Come Werner, you shall eat with me.

WERNER. Here in the inn? I shouldn't enjoy a bite.

TELLHEIM. No, in my room.

WERNER. I'll follow you at once, but first I want a word
with the little lady.

TELLHEIM. I should be delighted. (*Exit.*)

SCENE ELEVEN

PAUL WERNER *and* FRANZISKA

FRANZISKA. Well, sergeant major? . . .

WERNER. Little lady, when I come back again, shall I
get dressed up too?

FRANZISKA. Come as you please, sergeant major, my eyes
won't hold anything against you. But my ears will
have to be all the more on their guard . . . Twenty
fingers, and all full of rings! Eh, sergeant major?

WERNER. No, little lady, that was just what I wanted to
tell you. That cock-and-bull story just slipped out.
There's nothing in it. I think one ring is enough for
anybody. And I've heard the major say hundreds and
hundreds of times that he's a rotten kind of soldier
that would lead a girl on. And that's what I think
too, little lady. Rely on it! Now I must go after him.
Goodbye, little lady!

SCENE TWELVE

MINNA *and* FRANZISKA

MINNA. Has the major gone again? Franziska, I think
I am now calm enough for him to have stayed.

FRANZISKA. And I can make you a bit more calm.

MINNA. So much the better. His letter, oh, his letter! Every line told me what an honorable, noble man he is. Every refusal to accept me spoke of his love for me. I suppose he noticed that we'd read the letter. It doesn't matter as long as he comes. He is coming, isn't he? Perhaps a little too much pride in his behavior, Franziska. Not wanting to owe his good fortune to his beloved is pride, unforgivable pride. If I found too much pride in him, Franziska . . .

FRANZISKA. You'd give him up?

MINNA. So you're feeling sorry for him again already? No, my dear, you don't give up a man because of one flaw; but I have thought of a trick to give him some of his own medicine.

FRANZISKA. Oh, you must really be very calm, madam, if you're thinking of playing tricks again.

MINNA. I am; but come, you have a part to play in this as well.

ACT FOUR

SCENE ONE

MINNA's *boudoir*

MINNA, *richly but tastefully dressed and* FRANZISKA. *They are just getting up from the table, which is being cleared by a* SERVANT

FRANZISKA. You surely can't have had enough to eat, madam?

MINNA. Don't you think so, Franziska? Perhaps I wasn't hungry when I sat down at the table.

FRANZISKA. We had agreed not to mention him during the meal; perhaps we ought to have undertaken not to think of him as well.

MINNA. You're right. I was thinking of nothing but him.

FRANZISKA. I noticed that. I started to talk about a hundred different things, and each time you answered me absurdly. (*A second* SERVANT *enters with coffee.*) Dear, melancholy coffee.

MINNA. Caprices? I have none. I am just thinking about the lesson I'm going to give him. Do you understand what to do, Franziska?

FRANZISKA. Oh yes, but it would be better if he saved us the trouble.

MINNA. You'll see that I know him through and through. The man who refuses me when he thinks I am wealthy will fight the whole world for me when he learns that I am poor and forlorn.

FRANZISKA, *very earnestly*. And a thing like that must tickle even the most sensitive egotism.

MINNA. Don't moralize. You used to catch me out in vanity, now it's egotism. Now just leave me alone, dear Franziska. You ought to be able to wrap your sergeant major round your little finger, too.

FRANZISKA. My sergeant major?

MINNA. Yes, even if you deny it, it's still true. I haven't seen him yet, but from all that you've said about him, I'd prophesy that you are going to marry him.

SCENE TWO

RICCAUT DE LA MARLINIÈRE, MINNA, *and* FRANZISKA

RICCAUT, *offstage*. *Est-il permis, monsieur le Major?*

FRANZISKA. What is that? Is it coming to us? (*Moves toward the door.*)

RICCAUT. *Parbleu!* I 'ave made ze mistake . . . *Mais non* . . . I 'ave not made ze mistake . . . *C'est sa chambre.*

FRANZISKA. Madam, this man obviously thinks that Major von Tellheim is still here.

RICCAUT. Zat eez right. *Le Major de Tellheim; juste, ma belle enfant, c'est lui que je cherche. Où est-il?*

FRANZISKA. He doesn't live here any longer.

RICCAUT. *Comment?* Before twenty-four hour 'e is 'ere. And eez not staying any longer? Ver 'e stay?

MINNA, *coming up to him*. Sir . . .

RICCAUT. *Ah, madame . . . mademoiselle . . .* Your Grace, forgive . . .

MINNA. Sir, your mistake is a pardonable one, and your surprise quite natural. The major was kind enough to give up his room to me, as a stranger who did not know where she could find accommodation.

RICCAUT. *Ah, voilà de ses politesses! C'est un très galant homme que ce major.*

MINNA. I am ashamed to say that I do not know where he has gone in the meantime.

RICCAUT. Your Grace not know? *C'est dommage; j'en suis fâché.*

MINNA. I should have made enquiries. I am quite sure that his friends will go on looking for him here.

RICCAUT. I am very much of 'is friend, Your Grace.

MINNA. Franziska, do you know perhaps?

FRANZISKA. No, madam.

RICCAUT. I am needing to speak wis 'im. I come to bring 'im a *nouvelle* which will make 'im very 'appy.

MINNA. That makes me even more sorry; but I hope to speak to him myself, perhaps soon. If it is not important from whose mouth he hears this news, then I am happy to offer my services, sir.

RICCAUT. I understand. *Mademoiselle parle français? Mais sans doute; telle que je la vois! La demande etait bien impolie; Vous me pardonnerez, mademoiselle.*

MINNA. Sir . . .

RICCAUT. No? You are not speaking French?

MINNA. Sir, in France I would try to speak it. But why should I do so here? I can tell that you understand me, and I also understand you. You may speak however you like.

RICCAUT. Good, good! I can myself explain in German too. *Saches donc, mademoiselle* . . . I must tell Your Grace that I come from eating wis ze minister . . . minister of . . . minister of . . . 'ow eez calling 'imself ze minister . . . in ze long street . . . on ze big square?

MINNA. I am a complete stranger here.

RICCAUT. Well, ze minister of ze War Department. I dine zere at midday . . . I dine *à l'ordinaire* wis 'im . . . and zen we start to talk about Major Tellheim; *et le ministre m'a dit en confidence, car son Excellence est de mes amis, et il n'y a point de mystères entre nous* . . . 'Is Excellency, vat I vish to say, 'as told me in confidence, zat ze case of our major eez on ze point of ending. And ending good. 'E 'as made a report to ze king, and ze king 'as resolved *tout à fait en faveur du major.* "*Monsieur,*" *m'a dit son Excellence,* "*vous comprenez bien, que tout dépend de la manière, dont on fait envisager les choses au Roi, et vous me connaissez. Celà fait un très joli garçon que ce Tellheim, et ne sais-je pas que vous l'aimez? Les amis de mes amis sont aussi les miens. Il coûte un peu cher au Roi ce Tellheim, mais est-ce que l'on sert les rois pour rien? Il faut s'entr'aider en ce monde; et quand il s'agit de pertes, que ce soit le roi, qui en fasse, et non pas un honnête-homme de nous autres. Voilà le principe, dont je ne me dépars jamais.*" Vot say Your Grace? Is 'e not a good man? *Ah! que son Excellence a le coeur bien placé!* 'E assured me *au reste,* zat if ze major 'as not already received *une lettre de la main*—a letter from ze royal 'and—zat 'e must *infailliblement* receive one today.

MINNA. Indeed, sir, this news will be most welcome to Major von Tellheim. I only wish that I might tell him the name of the friend who is taking such an interest in his good fortune.

RICCAUT. Your Grace vish my name? *Vous voyez en moi* . . . Your Grace see in me *le Chevalier Riccaut de la Marlinière, Seigneur de Prêt-au-vol, de la Branche de Prensd'or.* Your Grace is very surprised zat I come from such a great family, *qui est véritablement du sang royal* . . . *Il faut le dire; je suis sans doute le cadet le plus aventureux, que la maison a jamais eu* . . . I am serving since I am eleven years old. An *affaire d'honneur* forced me to run avay. Zen I served 'Is 'Oliness, ze Pope, ze Republic of San Merino, ze crown of Poland, and in 'Olland, till at last I come 'ere. *Ah, mademoiselle, que je voudrais n'avoir jamais vu ce pays-là.* If only I could 'ave stayed in 'Olland, zen I would be now a colonel. But 'ere I remain a *capitaine*, and now a discharged *capitaine*.

MINNA. That's a great misfortune.

RICCAUT. *Oui, mademoiselle, me voilà reformé, et par la mis sur le pavé!*

MINNA. I am very sorry.

RICCAUT. *Vous êtes bien bonne, mademoiselle*, but as ze proverb goes, each misfortune brings 'is brother wis 'im; *qu'un malheur ne vient jamais seul*; zat is what 'appens to me. What can an *honnête-homme* of my *extraction* do for resources but to gamble? Always I 'ave played wis fortune, as long as I did not need fortune. But now I need 'er, *mademoiselle, je joue avec un guignon, qui surpasse toute croyance*. In ze last fifteen days, not a day 'as passed when I was not broken. Yesterday I was broken sree times. *Je sais bien, qu'il y avait quelque chose de plus que le jeu. Car parmi mes pontes se trouvaient certaines dames* . . . I say no more. You must be gallant to ze ladies. Zey invited me today, to give me *revanche; mais . . . vous m'entendez mademoiselle* . . . first you must earn ze living, before you can gamble.

MINNA. Sir, I will not hope . . .

RICCAUT. *Vous êtes bien bonne, mademoiselle* . . .

MINNA, *taking* FRANZISKA *aside*. Franziska, I really am sorry for this man. Do you think he would be offended if I offered him something?

FRANZISKA. He doesn't look as though he would.

MINNA. Good! . . . Sir, I hear . . . that you gamble, that you keep the bank, doubtless at places where there is something to be won. I must confess to you that I too . . . like to gamble . . .

RICCAUT. *Tant mieux, mademoiselle, tant mieux! Tous les gens d'esprit aiment le jeu à la fureur.*

MINNA. And to confess to you that I like to win and to entrust my money to one who . . . knows how to gamble. Would you have any interest, sir, in taking me into partnership? To grant me a share of your bank?

RICCAUT. *Comment, mademoiselle, vous voulez être de moitié avec moi? De tout mon coeur.*

MINNA. To begin with, just a bagatelle . . . (*She goes and takes money from her strongbox.*)

RICCAUT. *Ah, mademoiselle, que vous êtes charmante!*

MINNA. Here is something I won a short time ago, fifty talers . . . I must say that I am ashamed it is not more . . .

RICCAUT. *Donnez toujours, mademoiselle, donnez.* (*Takes the money.*)

MINNA. Of course, I have no doubt that your gaming house is a very respected one . . .

RICCAUT. Oh, very respected. Fifty talers? Your Grace shall 'ave a sird interest, *pour le tiers*—per'aps a little more. But wis a beautiful lady we do not take zings too precisely. I congratulate me to 'ave come into *liaison* with Your Grace, *et de ce moment je recommence à bien augurer de ma fortune.*

MINNA. But, unfortunately, I shall not be able to be present when you are playing, sir.

RICCAUT. Why does Your Grace need to be present? We gamblers are honest people among one anozer . . .

MINNA. If we are lucky, sir, then I shall expect you to return my portion, but if we have bad fortune . . .

RICCAUT. Zen I come and get some new recruits, eh, Your Grace?

MINNA. The recruits may run out if it goes on too long. So guard your money well, sir.

RICCAUT. What does Your Grace take me for? A simpleton, a block'ead?

MINNA. Forgive me, sir . . .

RICCAUT. *Je suis des bons, mademoiselle. Savez vous ce que celà veut dire?* I 'ave experience . . .

MINNA. But nevertheless, sir . . .

RICCAUT. *Je sais monter un coup* . . .

MINNA, *astonished*. But should you?

RICCAUT. *Je file une carte avec une adresse* . . .

MINNA. Never!

RICCAUT. *Je fais sauter la coupe avec une dextérité* . . .

MINNA. But sir, you surely wouldn't?

RICCAUT. Why not, Your Grace, why not? *Donnez moi un pigeonneau à plumer, et* . . .

MINNA. Play false? Cheat?

RICCAUT. *Comment, mademoiselle? Vous appelez cela* "cheat"? *Corriger la fortune, l'enchaîner sous ses doigts, être sûr de son fait*, is zat what ze Germans call "cheat"? "Cheat"! Oh, what a poor language German is, what a crude language!

MINNA. No, sir, if that is the way you think . . .

RICCAUT. *Laissez-moi faire, mademoiselle*, and do not worry. Why should you worry 'ow I play? Zat's enough, either Your Grace will see me tomorrow wis five hundred talers, or you never see me again . . . *Votre très humble, mademoiselle, votre très humble* . . . (*Hurries out.*)

MINNA, *looking after him with astonishment and displeasure*. I hope it will be the latter, sir, I hope it will be the latter!

SCENE THREE

MINNA *and* FRANZISKA

FRANZISKA, *bitterly*. I'm dumbfounded! Oh, beautiful, beautiful!

MINNA. All right, jeer at me, I deserve it. (*She pauses and then continues more calmly.*) Don't jeer at me, Franziska, I don't deserve it.

FRANZISKA. Marvellous, you've really done a kind act, you put a rogue back on his feet!

MINNA. I thought I was helping out an unfortunate.

FRANZISKA. And the funny thing is, the rogue thinks you're another of his sort . . . I must go after him and get the money back from him. (*Starts to leave.*)

MINNA. Franziska, don't let the coffee get completely cold. Pour me a cup.

FRANZISKA. He must give it back to you. You've changed your mind; you don't want to go into partnership with him. Fifty talers! You heard him say, madam, that he was a beggar. (MINNA *meanwhile pours out her own coffee.*) Whoever would give that much money to a beggar? And at the same time try to spare him the indignity of having had to beg for it? The generous man who pretends, out of his generosity, not to recognize a beggar is in his turn not recognized by the beggar. How would you like it, madam, if he looks on your gift as . . . I don't know what . . . (MINNA *gives her a cup of coffee.*) Are you trying to get me even more worked up? I don't want anything to drink. (MINNA *removes the cup.* FRANZISKA *imitates* RICCAUT.) "*Parbleu,* Your Grace, one 'as no recognition 'ere for eez service." Of course not, when they let rogues like that go running around loose without hanging them.

MINNA, *cold and meditative, while drinking.* My dear girl, you have such sympathy for good people, but when are you going to learn to put up with the bad ones? After all, they are people too . . . and often not nearly such bad people as they seem to be. You simply have to find their good side. I imagine that this Frenchman is nothing worse than vain. It's sheer vanity which makes him pretend to be a cheat. He doesn't want to feel obliged to me; he doesn't want to have to thank me. Perhaps he'll go and pay off some

of his small debts and live on what's left, as long as it
holds out, quietly and frugally, without a thought
about gambling. If that's the case, then let him fetch
his recruits whenever he wants to. (*Hands her the
cup.*) Here, put it away. But tell me, shouldn't
Tellheim be here by now?

FRANZISKA. No, madam, I can't do either. I can't find a
bad side to a good person or a good side to a bad one.

MINNA. But he is really coming?

FRANZISKA. He'd do better to stay away! Just because you
see a little pride in him, the best of men, you want to
play such a cruel trick on him?

MINNA. Are you back on that subject again? Say no
more; that's the way I want it to be. Don't spoil the
game for me. If you don't do exactly as I told you and
say exactly what I told you to say, I'll leave you alone
with him, and then . . . That must be him now.

SCENE FOUR

PAUL WERNER, *rather stiffly*, MINNA, *and* FRANZISKA

FRANZISKA. No, it's just his dear sergeant major.

MINNA. *Dear* sergeant major? What's all this about *dear*?

FRANZISKA. Madam, please don't confuse him. Your
servant, sergeant major, what have you brought for
us?

WERNER, *ignoring* FRANZISKA *and going directly to*
MINNA. Major von Tellheim asks me, sergeant major
Paul Werner, to pay his most humble respects to
Fräulein von Barnhelm and to tell her that he will be
here immediately.

MINNA. Where is he then?

WERNER. Your Grace will pardon him; we left our
quarters before the stroke of three, but the paymaster

general stopped us on the way, and since once you
start talking to people like that you never stop, he
gave me the nod to come and report the occurrence
to you.

MINNA. That's all right, sergeant major. I hope, though,
that the paymaster general had something pleasant
to say to the major.

WERNER. Officers like that very seldom do . . . Has Your
Grace any further orders? (*Starts to leave.*)

FRANZISKA. Where are you off to, sergeant major? I
thought we were going to have a little chat?

WERNER, *softly and seriously*. Not here, little lady, it's
not respectful and it would be insubordinate . . .
Madam . . .

MINNA. Thank you for your trouble, sergeant major. It
has been a great pleasure for me to meet you. Franziska has told me a lot of good things about you.
(WERNER *exits with a stiff bow.*)

SCENE FIVE

MINNA *and* FRANZISKA

MINNA. Is that your sergeant major, Franziska?

FRANZISKA. Since you mock me, I don't have time to
take you up on that "your" . . . Yes, madam, that is
my sergeant major. I'm sure that you find him a little
stiff and wooden. He even seemed that way to me just
now. But I noticed that in front of Your Grace he felt
as if he was on parade. And when soldiers are on
parade . . . they certainly do look more like marion-
ettes than men. But you ought to see and hear him
when he's on his own.

MINNA. Yes, I certainly ought.

FRANZISKA. He must still be outside, may I go and talk
to him for a while?

MINNA. You know how reluctant I am to deny you this
pleasure, but you must stay here, Franziska. You must .
be present while I am talking to the major. Oh, and
something else occurs to me. Take my ring and look
after it, and give me the major's. (*She takes her ring
off her finger.*)

FRANZISKA. Why?

MINNA, *while* FRANZISKA *is getting the other ring.* I
really don't know myself, but I have a feeling that I
might have a use for it . . . There's a knock . . . Give
it to me quickly! (*She puts it on.*) It's him!

SCENE SIX

TELLHEIM, *in the same uniform, but otherwise dressed as*
FRANZISKA *prescribed,* MINNA, *and* FRANZISKA

TELLHEIM. Madam, you will excuse my being late . . .

MINNA. Oh, major, we don't want to be quite that
military with one another. You are here, and looking
forward to a pleasure is a pleasure in itself! . . . Well?
(*She looks smilingly into his face.*) Dear Tellheim,
don't you think that we were being rather childish
earlier?

TELLHEIM. Yes, madam, it is childish to go on struggling
when you should resign yourself.

MINNA. I thought we might go for a drive, major . . .
take a look at the city . . . and then go to meet my
uncle.

TELLHEIM. What?

MINNA. You see, we still have not had a chance to talk
to each other about the most important matters. Yes,
he arrives today. It is mere chance that I arrived a
day ahead of him.

TELLHEIM. The Count of Bruchsal, has he returned?

MINNA. The disturbances caused by the war drove him to Italy, but peace has brought him back home again... Don't worry, Tellheim, even if we thought previously that the greatest obstacle to our union would come from his side . . .

TELLHEIM. Our union?

MINNA. He is your friend. He has heard too many good things from too many people about you not to be. He is dying to meet the man who has been chosen by his only heir. He is coming as uncle, as guardian, as father, to give me to you.

TELLHEIM. Madam, why didn't you read my letter? Why didn't you wish to read it?

MINNA. Your letter? Oh, yes, I remember, you did send me one. What happened to that letter, Franziska? Did we or didn't we read it? What did you write to me, dear Tellheim?

TELLHEIM. Nothing but what honor bids me.

MINNA. Which was that you should not leave an honorable girl, who loves you, in the lurch. Certainly honor would bid you write that. I certainly should have read the letter. But what I have not read, I can hear.

TELLHEIM. Yes, you shall hear it . . .

MINNA. No, I don't even need to hear it. It is obvious. Could you be capable of so mean a trick as not to want me now? Don't you know that all my life I would be in disgrace? My fellow countrymen would point their fingers at me. "That's her," they would say. "That's Fräulein von Barnhelm, who thought that just because she was rich, she could get the brave Tellheim—as if brave men are to be bought!" That's what they would say, for my fellow countrymen are all jealous of me. They can't deny that I am wealthy, but they don't want to know that in addition I am really quite a good girl and worthy of a man. Isn't that right, Tellheim?

TELLHEIM. Yes, yes, madam, I know your compatriots. I'm sure they would envy you an officer who has been discharged, whose honor has been besmirched, and who is a cripple and a beggar into the bargain.

MINNA. And are you supposed to be all those things? I heard something of the sort, if I am not mistaken, this morning. This seems to be a mixture of good and bad. Let's look at each point more closely. You are discharged? So I have heard, but I thought that your regiment had simply been absorbed into another. Why didn't they keep a man of your merit?

TELLHEIM. What had to happen has happened. The authorities have convinced themselves that a soldier does very little out of love for them, not much more from a sense of duty, but everything from the standpoint of his own reputation. Why then should they feel that they owe him anything? Peace has made several people like me dispensable to them, and in the final analysis no one is indispensable.

MINNA. You talk like a man who finds that, for his part, the authorities are very easily dispensable. And certainly this was never more true than at this moment. I am grateful to the authorities that they have renounced their claim to a man whom I would very unwillingly have shared with them . . . I am your commander, Tellheim, you don't need any other master. I could scarcely have dreamt that I would have the good fortune to find you discharged . . . But you are not simply discharged; you are more. Now let's see, what else is there? You are a cripple, you said. Well (*she looks him up and down*), for a cripple you seem to be pretty straight and in one piece, you seem pretty strong and well. Tellheim, if you're going begging on the strength of the loss of your limbs, I predict that you'll get very little except from good-hearted girls like myself.

TELLHEIM. At the moment you sound mischievous rather than good-hearted, my dear Minna.

MINNA. And all I hear in your rebuff, is "dear Minna."— I don't want to poke fun anymore, because I'm aware that you are a partial cripple. A shot did take away some of the use of your right arm. But, taken all in all, it's not so bad . . . I shall be in less danger from your beatings.

TELLHEIM. Madam!

MINNA. What you want to say is that you have even less to fear from mine.

TELLHEIM. You wish to laugh, madam. I am only sorry that I cannot laugh with you.

MINNA. Why not? What do you have against laughter? Can one not be serious even when laughing? Dear major, laughter keeps us more reasonable than melancholy. The proof is here at hand. Your beloved, though laughing, judges your situation far more accurately than you do yourself. You say that your honor is besmirched because you have been discharged; you say that you are a cripple because you were shot in the arm. Is that right? Isn't this an exaggeration? And isn't it my view that all exaggerations are comic? I'll bet that if we look into this beggar nonsense, it will prove to have as little basis as the rest. You've probably lost your equipment two or three times; some of your funds may have disappeared from this or that bank; you probably have no hope of being repaid for this or that advance that you made while you were in the service—but are you a beggar because of this? Even if you had nothing left but what my uncle is bringing you . . .

TELLHEIM. Your uncle is bringing me nothing.

MINNA. Nothing but the ten thousand talers which you so generously advanced to our government.

TELLHEIM. If only you had read my letter, madam!

MINNA. Oh, very well, I did read it. But I am completely puzzled about what you said on this point. No one is going to try to make a crime out of what was a noble act . . . Please explain it to me.

TELLHEIM. You will remember, madam, that I had orders to collect the levy in all the districts of your region with the utmost severity, and in cash. I wished to spare myself this severity, and so I advanced the sum which was lacking.

MINNA. Yes, I remember. I loved you for this even though I had not yet met you.

TELLHEIM. Your government gave me its promissory note, and I wanted to include this among the debts which had to be settled when the armistice was signed. The note was acknowledged as valid, but my right to it was disputed. People sneered when I assured them that I had advanced the money in cash. They declared that it was a bribe from your government because I had so quickly agreed to the lowest possible sum for the levy. Thus the note was taken from me, and if it is paid, it will certainly not be paid to me. It is for this reason, madam, that I regard my honor as having been besmirched. Not for my discharge, which I should have asked for in any case had I not received it—Are you serious, madam? Why aren't you laughing? Ha! Ha! Ha! I'm laughing.

MINNA. Oh, stop this laughter Tellheim! I beg you! It is the terrible laughter of the misanthrope. No, you are not the man to regret a good act merely because it had bad effects. No, these evil effects cannot persist. The truth must come to light. My uncle's evidence, the evidence of our legislature . . .

TELLHEIM. Your uncle! Your legislature! Ha, ha, ha!

MINNA. Your laughter is killing me, Tellheim! If you believe in virtue and providence, Tellheim, then don't laugh. I've never heard curses more dreadful than

your laughter. And even at the worst, supposing you
are misunderstood here, you would not be misunderstood in Thuringia. No, we cannot, we shall not
misunderstand you, Tellheim. And if our legislature
has the least concept of honor, then I know what they
must do. But I'm foolish: why should that be necessary? Imagine, Tellheim, that you had lost the ten
thousand talers in one wild evening. The king was
your unlucky card, but the queen will be all the
more favorable. Providence, believe me, always in-
demnifies the man who is honorable, and very often
ahead of time. The deed, which first was to cost you
ten thousand talers, was the very thing that won me
for you. Without this deed I should never have been
eager to meet you. You know that I came uninvited
to the first party at which I thought I should find you.
I only came because of you. I came with the firm
intention of loving you—I loved you already—with
the firm intention of possessing you, even if I had
found you as black and ugly as the Moor of Venice.
You aren't as black and ugly, nor would you be so
jealous. But Tellheim, Tellheim, you do have a lot
in common with him. Oh, these wild inflexible men
who can fix their obstinate eyes on nothing but the
ghost of their honor and who steel themselves against
any other feeling!... Look at me, Tellheim! (TELL-
HEIM, *meanwhile, has been staring fixedly in front of
himself.*) What are you thinking about? Can't you
hear me?

TELLHEIM, *absent-mindedly.* Oh yes! But tell me,
madam, how did the Moor enter Venetian service?
Why did he sell his strength and his blood to a foreign
country?

MINNA, *shocked.* Where are you, Tellheim?... Now it
is time to leave. Come! (*She takes his arm.*) Franziska,
have them send the carriage round.

TELLHEIM, *breaking free from* MINNA *and following*
FRANZISKA. No, Franziska, I fear that I cannot have
the honor of accompanying Fräulein von Barnhelm.
Madam, I pray you, leave me today to my common-
sense, and excuse me. You are doing your best to
make me lose it. I shall resist as much as I can . . . but
since I still have some sense left, listen, madam, to the
firm resolve which I have made and from which
nothing in the world shall shake me. If there is not
still a lucky throw left for me in the game, if the
tables are not completely turned, if . . .

MINNA. I'm afraid I have to interrupt you, major . . .
We should have told him straightaway, Franziska.
You never remind me of anything . . . Our conversa-
tion would have been quite different if I had begun it
with the good news which the Chevalier de la Marlinière just brought you.

TELLHEIM. The Chevalier de la Marlinière? Who is
that?

FRANZISKA. He seems to be quite a good man, except . . .

MINNA. Silence, Franziska! He is also a discharged
officer who comes from service in Holland . . .

TELLHEIM. Oh, Lieutenant Riccaut!

MINNA. He assured me that he was your friend.

TELLHEIM. And I can assure you that I am not his.

MINNA. And that one of the ministers, I forget which,
had told him that your affair was close to a favorable
conclusion. Apparently a letter from the king is on its
way to you.

TELLHEIM. How on earth could Riccaut have been meet-
ing with a minister? It's true that something should
have been decided, because the paymaster general
just now told me that the king had dismissed all the
charges from the written parole which I gave not to
leave here until everything was settled. But that must
be all there is to it. They're simply going to let me go.

But they are mistaken; I shall not go. I would rather die in penury before the very eyes of my defamers . . .

MINNA. Obstinate man!

TELLHEIM. I need no grace; I seek justice. My honor . . .

MINNA. The honor of a man like you . . .

TELLHEIM, *with heat*. No, madam, you may be a good judge of everything else, but not of this. Honor is not the voice of conscience, not the testimony of those who are less noble . . .

MINNA. No, no, I know! Honor is . . . honor . . .

TELLHEIM. One moment, madam, you have not permitted me to say all that I had to . . . I wanted to say that if I am to be unscrupulously denied that which is mine, if I do not find complete satisfaction for my honor, then, madam, I cannot be yours. For in the eyes of the world, I am not worthy to be. Fräulein von Barnhelm deserves a man of irreproachable character. A love which allows its object to be the man who is not ashamed to depend upon a girl for his happiness, whose blind tenderness . . .

MINNA. Are you serious, major? (*Turning her back upon him.*) Franziska . . .

TELLHEIM. Don't be angry, madam.

MINNA, *aside to* FRANZISKA. Now is the moment! What do you advise, Franziska?

FRANZISKA. I advise nothing, but he is certainly making it hard for you.

TELLHEIM, *advancing to interrupt them*. You are angry, madam . . .

MINNA, *scornfully*. Me? Not in the least.

TELLHEIM. If I loved you less, madam . . .

MINNA, *in the same tone*. That would be my misfortune . . . And major, believe me, I do not wish to be your misfortune. We must remain unselfish in our love. It's just as well that I was not more open hearted. Perhaps your sympathy would have granted me what your heart denies. (*Slowly taking the ring from her finger.*)

TELLHEIM. What do you mean by that, madam?

MINNA. No, neither of us should make the other either more or less happy. That is the meaning of true love. I believe you, Tellheim, and you have too much honor not to recognize true love.

TELLHEIM. Are you laughing at me, madam?

MINNA. Here, take back the ring with which you pledged your love to me. (*Gives him the ring.*) There, now we'll pretend we never knew each other.

TELLHEIM. What are you saying?

MINNA. Why are you surprised? Take it, sir . . . You surely weren't playing coy?

TELLHEIM, *taking the ring from her hand.* Oh, God, can Minna talk like this?

MINNA. You cannot be mine in one case; I cannot be yours in any. Your misfortune is only apparent; mine is certain. (*Starts to exit.*)

TELLHEIM. Where are you going, my dearest Minna?

MINNA. Sir, you insult me now with this familiarity.

TELLHEIM. What is the matter, madam? Where are you going?

MINNA. Let me go. Let me hide my tears from you . . . traitor! (*Exits.*)

SCENE SEVEN

TELLHEIM *and* FRANZISKA

TELLHEIM. Her tears? And I am supposed to let her go. (*Starts to follow* MINNA.)

FRANZISKA, *restraining him.* Major, you surely wouldn't follow her into her bedroom?

TELLHEIM. Her misfortune, did she not speak of her misfortune?

FRANZISKA. Certainly. Her misfortune to lose you after . . .

TELLHEIM. After? After what? There's something else. What is it, Franziska? Speak, tell me . . .

FRANZISKA. After she . . . I wanted to say . . . had sacrificed so much for you.

TELLHEIM. Sacrificed? For me?

FRANZISKA. Listen, I will be quite brief. It is just as well, major, that you got rid of her in this manner . . . Why shouldn't I tell you? It can't remain secret much longer . . . We fled! . . . The Count of Bruchsal has disinherited my mistress because she would not accept a man of his choice. She has lost everything and renounced everything. What were we to do? We decided to search for the one who . . .

TELLHEIM. Enough! Come, I must throw myself at her feet.

FRANZISKA. What are you thinking about? You ought to thank your lucky stars . . .

TELLHEIM. Wretch! Whom do you take me for? No, dear Franziska, such advice did not come from your heart. Forgive me!

FRANZISKA. Don't delay me any longer. I must go and see what she is doing. How easily something might have happened to her! . . . Leave us. Come back later if you wish to. (*Exits to* MINNA.)

SCENE EIGHT

TELLHEIM

TELLHEIM. But Franziska! . . . I will await you here . . . No, this is more urgent! . . . If she sees how serious I am, she cannot refuse me her forgiveness . . . Now I do have need of you, honest Werner . . . No, Minna, I am not a traitor! (*Exit in haste.*)

ACT FIVE

SCENE ONE

The Parlor

TELLHEIM *from one side*, WERNER *from the other*.

TELLHEIM. Werner, I've been looking everywhere for you. Where have you been?

WERNER. And I've been looking for you, major. I bring you some good news.

TELLHEIM. It's not your news I need at the moment; I need your money. Hurry, Werner, give me as much as you have, and then go and see if you can borrow as much as possible!

WERNER. Major?... Bless my soul, didn't I say he'd only borrow from me when he had something to lend himself?

TELLHEIM. Surely you're not looking for excuses?

WERNER. So that I shall have nothing to reproach him with, he takes it with one hand and gives it back with the other.

TELLHEIM. Don't delay Werner! I certainly intend to repay, but when and how, God only knows!

WERNER. Then you don't know that the court treasury has received orders to pay you your money. I just heard from . . .

TELLHEIM. What are you talking about? Who are you letting fool you? Surely you must know that if it were

true, I would be the first to hear about it? Quickly,
Werner, money, money!

WERNER. By God! With pleasure! Here is some. The
five hundred talers and the three hundred. (*Hands him
both.*)

TELLHEIM. The five hundred talers! Go and get Just,
Werner. He's to redeem at once the ring which he
pawned this morning. But where are you going to get
more, Werner? I need a lot more.

WERNER. Let me worry about that. The man who
bought my farm lives in town. We were not due to
close for two weeks, but the money is there, and for a
half percent discount.

TELLHEIM. Very well, Werner. Don't you see that you
are my only source of refuge?... I must confide in
you completely ... The young lady here ... you saw
her ... is unhappy.

WERNER. That's bad.

TELLHEIM. But tomorrow she will be my wife.

WERNER. That's good.

TELLHEIM. And the day after tomorrow I shall leave with
her. I have permission to leave, and I wish to leave.
I would rather leave everything here in the lurch.
Who knows where else I may find good fortune? If
you like, Werner, come with me. We'll enlist again.

WERNER. Really?... But someplace where there's a
war on, major?

TELLHEIM. Where else? But go, my dear Werner, we'll
talk about this later.

WERNER. A major after my own heart! The day after
tomorrow? Why not, rather, tomorrow?... I'll get
everything in order ... Major, there's a wonderful
war in Persia! What do you think of that?

TELLHEIM. We'll think about it. Go now, Werner!

WERNER. Hurrah, hurrah! Long live Prince Heraclius!
(*Exit.*)

SCENE TWO

TELLHEIM

TELLHEIM. What has happened to me? My soul is newly inspired. My own misfortune cast me down, made me angry, short-sighted, shy, indolent. Her misfortune raises me up again. I look around again as a free man and feel the strength and the will to undertake everything for her . . . Why am I waiting? (*Is about to go to* MINNA's *room when* FRANZISKA *comes out.*)

SCENE THREE

FRANZISKA *and* TELLHEIM

FRANZISKA. So, it's you? I thought I heard your voice. What do you want, major?

TELLHEIM. What do I want? . . . What is your mistress doing? Come!

FRANZISKA. She's just going out.

TELLHEIM. Alone? Without me? Where is she going?

FRANZISKA. Have you forgotten, major?

TELLHEIM. Have you no sense, Franziska? I upset her and she was offended. I shall ask her forgiveness and she will forgive me.

FRANZISKA. What? After you took back the ring?

TELLHEIM. I did that without knowing what I was doing . . . I have just remembered the ring . . . Where did I put it? (*Looks for it.*) Here it is.

FRANZISKA. Is that it? (TELLHEIM *replaces the ring.*) (*Aside.*) If only he would look at it a little more closely.

TELLHEIM. She forced it on me with such bitterness . . . but I have forgotten this bitterness already. When you are under stress, you don't always weigh your words

very carefully. But she won't refuse for a moment to
take back the ring. And don't I still have hers?

FRANZISKA. She's expecting to get that back ... Where
is it, major? Show it to me.

TELLHEIM, *somewhat abashed.* I ... I forgot to bring it
with me ... Just ... Just is going to bring it to me at
once.

FRANZISKA. I suppose one is very much like the other.
Let me have a look at this one; I love looking at things
like that.

TELLHEIM. Another time, Franziska. Come ...

FRANZISKA, *aside.* He simply won't see his mistake.

TELLHEIM. What did you say? Mistake?

FRANZISKA. I meant to say that it is a mistake if you still
think my mistress is still a good match. Her own
estate is a very modest one, and her guardians could
reduce it to nothing by a few self-seeking calculations.
She expected to inherit everything from her uncle,
but this cruel uncle ...

TELLHEIM. Don't talk of him. Am I not man enough to
recompense her for everything?

FRANZISKA. Did you hear? She's ringing for me; I must
go in.

TELLHEIM. I'm going with you.

FRANZISKA. Oh for heaven's sake, no! She expressly
forbade me to talk to you. At least wait and come
after I have gone in.

SCENE FOUR

TELLHEIM

TELLHEIM, *calling after her.* Announce me to her!
Speak for me, Franziska! I'll come after you immediately! ... What shall I say to her? When you
speak from the heart, there is no need of preparation.

The one thing that might need careful handling is her reticence, her hesitation to throw herself into my arms because of her misfortune, her eagerness to pretend to a good fortune which she lost on my account. To excuse herself for this lack of trust in my honor, in her own value, to excuse herself . . . I have already excused it . . . Ah, but here she comes.

SCENE FIVE

MINNA, FRANZISKA, *and* TELLHEIM

MINNA, *coming out as though unaware of the major's presence*. The carriage is waiting, isn't it Franziska? . . . My fan, please.

TELLHEIM, *going up to her*. Where are you going, madam?

MINNA, *with affected coldness*. Out, major. I can guess the reason for your coming back here—to give me my ring back as well . . . Very well, major, please have the goodness to hand it to Franziska. Franziska, take the ring from the major! I'm afraid I have no time to lose. (*About to go.*)

TELLHEIM, *walking in front of her*. Madam! What's this I hear, madam? I am not worthy of such love?

MINNA. Well, Franziska, so you told the major . . .

FRANZISKA. Everything.

TELLHEIM. Please don't be angry with me, madam. I am no traitor. You have lost much on my account in the eyes of the world, but not in my own. In my eyes you have gained incalculably by this loss. It was all too new. You feared that you might make an unfavorable impression upon me. At first you wanted to conceal it from me. I don't complain about this lack of trust. I know that it came from your desire to keep me, and this desire is a source of pride to me. You

found that I too had suffered misfortune, and you
didn't want to pile misfortune upon misfortune. You
couldn't imagine how much more your misfortune
meant to me than my own.

MINNA. That's all well and good, major, but it has
happened once and for all. I have released you from
your obligation by taking back this ring.

TELLHEIM. I have agreed to nothing . . . indeed, I
regard myself as under a greater obligation than
before. You are mine, Minna, for ever mine! (*He
takes out the ring.*) Here, take for a second time this
pledge of my faithfulness.

MINNA. Me? Take this ring back? This ring?

TELLHEIM. Yes, dearest Minna, yes!

MINNA. What do you take me for? This ring?

TELLHEIM. The first time you took this ring from my
hand, our circumstances were equal and we both
enjoyed good fortune. They are no longer fortunate,
but they are at least equal again. Equality is always the
strongest bond of love. Allow, me, my dearest Minna
. . . (*Seizes her hand to place the ring on it.*)

MINNA. What, by force, major? No, there is no power in
the world which would make me take this ring back.
Do you think I have a need for rings? You see, don't
you, that I have one here which is not in the least
inferior to yours?

FRANZISKA. He still doesn't see it!

TELLHEIM, *letting* MINNA's *hand drop.* What does this
mean? I see Fräulein von Barnhelm, but it is not her
that I hear. You are playing coy, madam . . . Forgive
my imitating you and using this expression.

MINNA, *in her true tone.* Did this word insult you, major?

TELLHEIM. It hurt me.

MINNA, *touched.* It was not meant to, Tellheim . . .
Forgive me, Tellheim.

TELLHEIM. Thank God! This warmth of tone tells me

that you are coming to yourself, madam, that you love me, Minna.

FRANZISKA, *bursting out*. The joke almost went too far.

MINNA, *imperiously*. Please do not interfere, Franziska!

FRANZISKA, *aside and taken aback*. Still not enough?

MINNA. Yes, sir. It would be feminine vanity to remain cold and disdainful. Away with all that! You deserve to find in me someone just as truthful as you are yourself . . . I still love you, Tellheim, I still love you, but nevertheless . . .

TELLHEIM. No more, dearest Minna, no more! (*Seizes her hand again to put the ring on it.*)

MINNA, *withdrawing her hand*. But nevertheless . . . it is for this very reason that I can never again allow this to happen . . . never again! . . . What are you thinking about, major! I thought you had enough to think about with your own misfortune . . . You must remain here, you must extort the most complete satisfaction. In my haste I can think of no other word but extort . . . even if the most extreme misfortune were to consume you under the very eyes of your slanderers.

TELLHEIM. That was my first thought; that's what I said when I didn't know what I was saying and thinking. Vexation and stifled rage had clouded my whole soul. Love itself in the fullest splendor of good fortune could not dispel the gloom. But Love sent her daughter, Pity, who being more familiar with the blackness of pain, dispelled the clouds and opened my whole soul once again to impressions of tenderness. I felt the urge for self-preservation because I had something to preserve which was more valuable than myself and which had to be preserved by me. Please do not be insulted by this word "pity," madam. You can hear it without humiliation because it comes from the inno-cent cause of our misfortune. I am the cause. It is on my account, Minna, that you are losing friends and relatives, possessions and fatherland. And it is through me and in me that you must find all these again, or I shall have the ruin of the most lovable of your sex on my conscience. Please don't make me even think about a future in which I would have to hate myself . . . No, nothing shall keep me here any longer. From this moment on I shall show nothing but scorn for the injustice which has been meted out to me here. Is this country the whole world? Is this the only place where the sun rises? Where may I not go? Who will refuse me service even if I have to seek it under the farthest sky? Follow me with confidence, dearest Minna. We shall lack for nothing. I have a friend who will gladly help me . . .

SCENE SIX

An Orderly, Tellheim, Minna, *and* Franziska

Franziska, *catching sight of the* Orderly. Sh, Major!

Tellheim, *to the orderly*. Who are you looking for?

Orderly. I am looking for Major von Tellheim . . . Ah! So it's you. Sir, this royal letter (*he takes the letter out of his wallet*) I am to hand you.

Tellheim. For me?

Orderly. According to the address.

Minna. Franziska, do you hear? The chevalier was speaking the truth after all!

Orderly, *as* Tellheim *takes the letter*. I must beg your pardon, sir. You would have received it yesterday, but it was impossible to find you. It was only today on parade that I learned your address from Lieutenant Riccaut.

Franziska. Madam, did you hear? . . . This is the chevalier's minister . . . "'Ow is calling 'imself ze minister on ze big square?"

TELLHEIM. I am most grateful to you for your trouble.
ORDERLY. It is my pleasure, major.

SCENE SEVEN

TELLHEIM, MINNA, *and* FRANZISKA

TELLHEIM. Madam, what do I have here? What are the
contents of this letter?
MINNA. I have no right to extend my curiosity so far.
TELLHEIM. What, do you still think of your fate as
separate from mine? ... But why am I waiting to
open it? It can scarcely make me more unhappy than
I am now. No, dearest Minna, it cannot make us more
unhappy ... but perhaps it can make us happier!
Permit me, madam. (*Opens the dispatch and reads it.
The* LANDLORD *enters.*)

SCENE EIGHT

LANDLORD, TELLHEIM, MINNA, *and* FRANZISKA

LANDLORD, *to Franziska.* Psst, my dear, a word!
FRANZISKA, *going up to him.* Sir? I'm afraid we don't
know ourselves what's in the letter.
LANDLORD. Who wants to know about the letter?
I've come about the ring. Your mistress must return
it to me at once. Just is here and wants to redeem it.
MINNA, *who has also come up to the* LANDLORD. Tell Just
that the ring has already been redeemed; and tell him
by whom—by me.
LANDLORD. But ...

MINNA. I take full responsibility. You may go! (*Exit* LANDLORD.)

SCENE NINE

TELLHEIM, MINNA, *and* FRANZISKA

FRANZISKA. And now, madam, it's time to stop teasing the major.

MINNA. Stop your pleading! Don't you know that the knot will untie itself at any moment?

TELLHEIM, *after reading the letter with the most lively show of emotion.* Ah, here, too, he has revealed his true self ... Oh, madam, what justice! ... what grace! ... This is more than I had expected ... more than I deserve ... My fortune, my honor, everything is restored. Surely, I am still dreaming! (*Looking once more at the letter as though to reassure himself.*) No, it is not an illusion called forth by my own wishes ... Read it for yourself, madam, read it for yourself!

MINNA. I would not be so presumptuous, major.

TELLHEIM. Presumptuous? The letter is to me, to your Tellheim, Minna. It contains ... something that your uncle cannot take away from you. You must read it; please read it!

MINNA. If, in so doing, I do you a favor, major ... (*She takes the letter and reads it.*)

"My dear Major Tellheim:

We hereby inform you that the matter which had given us concern for your honor has been explained to your advantage. Our brother was informed of it in greater detail, and his evidence has shown you to be innocent. The treasury has orders to restore to you the letters of credit which were called into question and to repay the advances which you made. We have also commanded that all claims which the paymaster had

against you be dismissed. Please inform us if your
state of health permits you to take up service again.
We would not readily wish to lose a man of your
courage and temper.

> Your most affectionate Majesty, etc."

TELLHEIM. What do you have to say to that?

MINNA, *folding up the letter and returning it to him.* I?
Nothing.

TELLHEIM. Nothing?

MINNA. Well, yes: that your king is a great man and
probably also a good man . . . But that is no concern of
mine. He is not my king.

TELLHEIM. And do you have nothing else to say?
Nothing about us?

MINNA. You are going back into his service. The major
will become a lieutenant colonel, perhaps a full
colonel. I give you my heartiest congratulations.

TELLHEIM. Do you not know me better than that? No,
since fortune is restoring so much to me—more
than enough to satisfy the wishes of any reasonable
man—it will depend entirely upon Minna whether
or not I belong to anyone else but her. May my whole
life be devoted to your service! It is dangerous to
serve the mighty, and such service offers no recompense for the humiliation and the duress which it
brings. Minna is not one of those vain women who
only love their men for their title and rank. She will
love me for myself, and for her sake I shall renounce
the rest of the world. I became a soldier because of a
certain partisanship. I do not know, myself, the
political principles for which I fought. And it was a
whim of mine that soldiering is good for every man of
honor for a time at least, so that he may become
familiar with everything that men call danger and so
learn boldness and determination. Only the most
extreme necessity could have compelled me to make a

vocation out of this experiment, to make a profession out of this temporary occupation. But now that I am no longer under any sort of pressure, now my total ambition is to be a peaceful and contented human being. With you, dearest Minna, that is what I shall surely become. That is what, in your company, I shall constantly remain . . . May the most holy bond of matrimony join us tomorrow, and then we will search throughout the whole wide world for the most peaceful, pleasing, and delightful corner, which has all that is needed for a true paradise except a loving couple. There we will live; there shall all of our days . . . What is the matter, Minna? (MINNA *moves uneasily back and forth, trying to conceal her emotion.*)

MINNA, *pulling herself together.* You are cruel, Tellheim, to describe so attractively a happiness which you know I must reject. My loss . . .

TELLHEIM. Your loss? What do you mean by your loss? Anything which Minna could lose would not be Minna's. You are the sweetest, loveliest, most enchanting creature under the sun, full of goodness and generosity, full of innocence and happiness . . . mixed now and then with a little wantonness, perhaps, and now and again a touch of obstinacy . . . But so much the better! So much the better! Otherwise, Minna would be an angel whom I should have to worship with awe, whom I could not love. (*Takes her hand to kiss it.*)

MINNA, *taking her hand back.* No, sir! . . . What is this change which has suddenly come over you? Is this flattering, tempestuous lover the cold Tellheim? Could only the return of his fortune kindle these fires in him? I trust that you will permit me in these sudden fits of heat and cold to preserve a little judgement for both of us. When he himself was in a position to turn things over in his mind, he said that it was an

unworthy love which did not hesitate to subject its
object to scorn . . . That is so, but I too am seeking a
love which is as pure and noble as his . . . And now
that honor summons him, now that a great king seeks
his favor, am I to allow him to give himself up to
dreams of love with me? And have the famous warrior
degenerate into a dallying swain? . . . No, sir, follow
the summons of your own better fate.

TELLHEIM. Very well, then, if you find the big world
more attractive Minna . . . good, then let us remain in
the big world! . . . How insignificant, how poor this
big world is! You know it only from its tinsel side. But
in truth, Minna, you will . . . Never mind! Until that
time, all right! There will be no lack of admirers for
your perfection and no lack of people jealous of my
good fortune.

MINNA. No, Tellheim, that's not what I meant. I'm
directing you back into the big world, back to the path
of your honor, but I don't wish to follow you . . . In
that world, Tellheim needs a wife who is beyond
reproach. A girl from Saxony who has thrown herself
into his arms . . .

TELLHEIM, *starting up and looking wildly around him.*
Who dares to talk like that? . . . Minna, I tremble
when I think that anyone but you should have said
this. My rage against him would have known no
bounds.

MINNA. You see, that's what I fear. You would not
suffer the smallest piece of ridicule about me, but day
in and day out you would have to put up with the
most bitter mockery. In short, Tellheim, listen to the
decision which I have made and from which nothing
in the world will shake me.

TELLHEIM. Before you finish, madam . . . I beg you,
Minna . . . think for a moment that you are passing a
verdict of life or death on me.

MINNA. Without a further thought . . . as surely as I gave

you back the ring with which you once pledged me your faith, and as surely as you took this same ring back, so surely shall the unfortunate Barnhelm never become the wife of the more fortunate Tellheim.

TELLHEIM. And this is your sentence, madam?

MINNA. Equality is the only firm bond of love. The fortunate Barnhelm wished to live only for the fortunate Tellheim. Even the unhappy Minna might have let herself be persuaded to increase or decrease the misfortune of her friend . . . He must have noticed, before this letter came to make us unequal once more, how my refusal was only feigned.

TELLHEIM. Is that true, madam? . . . I thank you, Minna, that you have not passed the final sentence . . . Is it only the unfortunate Tellheim that you want? He can be had. (*Coldly.*) I have the feeling that it is not right for me to accept this long-overdue vindication; that it might be better if I did not seek the return of that which has so shamefully been taken from my honor . . . Yes, I will pretend not to have received the letter. That shall be my answer! (*About to tear the letter up.*)

MINNA, *taking his hand.* What are you going to do, Tellheim?

TELLHEIM. Possess you.

MINNA. Wait!

TELLHEIM. Madam, I swear to you that I shall tear it up unless you change your mind. Then we shall see what further objections you have.

MINNA. What, in this tone? . . . Have I to grow despicable in my own eyes? Never! Only a worthless creature would not be shamed to owe her whole good fortune to the blind tenderness of a man.

TELLHEIM. False, absolutely false!

MINNA. Surely you don't dare deny your own words when they come from my lips?

TELLHEIM. Sophistry! Will the weaker sex be dishonored

by everything which is unsuited to the stronger? May a man permit himself what a woman does? Which sex was determined by nature to be the support of the other?

MINNA. Calm yourself, Tellheim! I shall not be completely without protection . . . even if I have to reject the honor of yours. My needs will still be attended to. I have called upon our ambassador. He wishes to talk to me today. I hope that he will take me under his protection. But the time is getting on. Permit me, major . . .

TELLHEIM. I will accompany you, madam.

MINNA. No, sir, leave me.

TELLHEIM. Your shadow shall leave you before I do. Come, madam, we will go where you want, to whom you want. Everywhere, a hundred times a day and in your presence, I shall tell friends and strangers alike of the bond which holds you to me, and of the cruel obstinacy which makes you want to break these bonds.

SCENE TEN

JUST, TELLHEIM, MINNA, *and* FRANZISKA

JUST, *rushing in.* Major! Major!

TELLHEIM. Yes?

JUST. Come quickly, quickly!

TELLHEIM. Why? Come here! Tell me, what is it?

JUST. Listen . . . (*Whispers to* TELLHEIM.)

MINNA, *aside to* FRANZISKA. Do you notice anything, Franziska?

FRANZISKA. Oh, you are a merciless creature! I have been on tenterhooks.

TELLHEIM, *to* JUST. What did you say? . . . It's impossible! . . . You? (*Looking wildly at* MINNA.) Say it out loud, say it to her face . . . Listen, madam!

JUST. The landlord says that Fräulein von Barnhelm has redeemed the ring which I pawned. She recognized it as her own and refused to give it back.

TELLHEIM. Is this true, madam? No, it can't be true!

MINNA, *smiling*. And why can't it be true, Tellheim?

TELLHEIM, *passionately*. All right, it is true! A terrible light suddenly dawns upon me . . . Now I recognize you, false, faithless one!

MINNA. *frightened*. Who? Who is faithless?

TELLHEIM. You, whom I can no longer name by name.

MINNA. Tellheim!

TELLHEIM. Forget my name! You came here to break with me, that much is clear . . . and chance played into your hands! It restored the ring to you, and by your own trickery you made me take my own ring back.

MINNA. Tellheim, what ghosts are you conjuring up? Pull yourself together and listen to me.

FRANZISKA, *to herself*. Now she'll get it!

SCENE ELEVEN

WERNER, *with a purse*, TELLHEIM, MINNA, FRANZISKA, *and* JUST

WERNER. Here I am back already, major!

TELLHEIM, *without looking at him*. Who sent for you?

WERNER. Here's money, five thousand talers.

TELLHEIM. I don't want it!

WERNER. Tomorrow, sir, you can have the same amount again if you want it.

TELLHEIM. Keep your money!

WERNER. It's your money, sir. I don't think you know who you're talking to.

TELLHEIM. Take it away, I say!

WERNER. What's the matter? I'm Paul Werner.

TELLHEIM. All goodness is sheer hypocrisy, all kindness mere deceit.

WERNER. Is that true of me?

TELLHEIM. Just as you like!

WERNER. I only carried out orders.

TELLHEIM. Then carry out this one as well, and be off!

WERNER. Sir! (*Angry.*) I am a man . . .

TELLHEIM. That's something to be proud of!

WERNER. Who has something of a temper . . .

TELLHEIM. Good! Temper is the best thing we have.

WERNER. Please, sir . . .

TELLHEIM. How often do I have to tell you? I don't need your money!

WERNER, *angry*. All right, then, let him have it who wants it! (*He throws the purse down and goes to one side.*)

MINNA. Oh, Franziska, my dear, I should have followed your advice. I've carried the joke too far . . . But he only needs to listen to me . . . (*Going up to him.*)

FRANZISKA. Sergeant major!! (*She has moved up to him without answering* MINNA.)

WERNER, *angry*. Go away!

FRANZISKA. Ugh! What sort of men are these?

MINNA. Tellheim! Tellheim! (TELLHEIM *is biting his fingers in rage and has turned away from* MINNA, *refusing to listen to her.*) I went too far! . . . Listen to me! . . . You are deceiving yourself . . . a sheer misunderstanding . . . Tellheim! . . . Won't you listen to your Minna? . . . Can you nurse such a suspicion? . . . I wanted to break with you? . . . And that's the reason I came here? . . . Tellheim!

SCENE TWELVE

Two SERVANTS (*they enter from opposite sides and run across the room*), WERNER, TELLHEIM, MINNA, FRANZISKA, *and* JUST

FIRST SERVANT. Madam, His Excellency, the count!

SECOND SERVANT. He is coming, madam!

FRANZISKA, *runs to the window.* It's him, it's him!

MINNA. Is it him? . . . Hurry, Tellheim, hurry!

TELLHEIM, *suddenly coming to himself.* Who, who's coming? Your uncle, madam? This cruel uncle? All right, let him come, let him! Have no fear! He shall not harm you with so much as a glance. He has me to reckon with . . . It's true that you don't deserve it of me . . .

MINNA. Oh, hurry, Tellheim! Put your arms around me and forget everything . . .

TELLHEIM. If only I thought you might regret your treatment of me!

MINNA. No, I cannot regret having caught a glimpse of your whole heart! . . . What a wonderful man you are! Put your arms around your Minna, your happy Minna, and happy most of all on your account. (*She falls into his arms.*) And now, let's go to meet him . . .

TELLHEIM. Meet whom?

MINNA. The best of your unknown friends.

TELLHEIM. What?

MINNA. The count, my uncle, my father, your father . . . My flight, his anger, my disinheritance . . . don't you know that it was all made up? How gullible you are, my dear!

TELLHEIM. Made up? But the ring? The ring?

MINNA. Where is the ring I gave back to you?

TELLHEIM. You'll take it back? . . . How happy you make me! . . . Here, Minna! (*Takes it out.*)

MINNA. Look at it first . . . Oh, there's none so blind as

those who won't see! . . . Which ring is it? The one I
had from you or the one you had from me?—Isn't it
the very one I didn't wish to leave in the landlord's
hands?

TELLHEIM. My God, what is this? What are you saying?

MINNA. Shall I take it back now? Shall I? . . . Give it to
me, give it to me! (*She takes it from his hand and
places it on his finger.*) Now, is everything all right?

TELLHEIM. Where am I? . . . (*Kisses her hand.*) Oh, you
wicked angel! To torture me like that! . . .

MINNA. This was just a proof, my dear husband, that you
can never play a trick on me without my playing one
on you immediately after. Don't you think that you
tortured me as well?

TELLHEIM. You actresses! I should have known you
better than that.

FRANZISKA. No, really, I don't think I could be an actress.
I was trembling and shuddering and had to hold my
hand to my mouth to keep it shut.

MINNA. My role didn't come easily to me either. But
come!

TELLHEIM. I still can't get over it . . . How well I feel,
yet how frightened! It's like waking from a night-
mare.

MINNA. We're delaying. I hear him.

SCENE THIRTEEN

COUNT OF BRUCHSAL, *accompanied by* LANDLORD,
MINNA, FRANZISKA, TELLHEIM, JUST, WERNER, *and*
SERVANTS

COUNT. You arrived safely, then?

MINNA, *going towards him.* Ah, father! . . .

COUNT. Yes, here I am, my dearest Minna. (*He puts his
arms round her.*) But what's this, girl? (*Seeing* TELL-

HEIM.) You've only been here twenty-four hours, and you've already made some acquaintances and are beginning to entertain?

MINNA. Can you guess who it is?

COUNT. Surely not your Tellheim?

MINNA. Who else but him? . . . Come, Tellheim! (*She takes him to the* COUNT.)

COUNT. Sir, we have never made each other's acquaintance, and yet I thought I recognized you as soon as I saw you. I hoped it might be you. Come, embrace me . . . You enjoy my deepest respect. I ask your friendship . . . My niece, my daughter, loves you.

MINNA. Do you know that, father? . . . And is my love blind?

COUNT. No, Minna, your love is not blind, but your beloved . . . is mute.

TELLHEIM, *going into his arms*. Please let me pull myself together, father.

COUNT. Very well, my son. I hear that, even if your mouth cannot speak, your heart can. As a rule I do not care for officers who wear this color (*points to* TELL-HEIM's *uniform*), but you are an honest man, Tellheim, and an honest man can wear what he likes; people will still like him.

MINNA. If only you knew everything!

COUNT. But why shouldn't I learn everything? . . . Where are my rooms landlord?

LANDLORD. If Your Excellency would do me the honor of stepping this way.

COUNT. Come, Minna! Come, sir! (*Exit with* LANDLORD *and* SERVANTS.)

MINNA. Come, Tellheim!

TELLHEIM. I'll follow you in a minute, madam. Just one more word with this man here. (*Turns to* WERNER.)

MINNA. And make it a good one. I think you owe it to him. Right, Franziska?

SCENE FOURTEEN

TELLHEIM, WERNER, JUST, *and* FRANZISKA

TELLHEIM, *pointing to the purse which* WERNER *has just thrown away*.) Here, Just, pick up that purse and take it home. Go on! (JUST *picks it up and exits*.)

WERNER, *who has been standing angrily in the corner and not participating in any of the foregoing*. Well?

TELLHEIM, *going up to him confidentially*. Werner, when can I have the other five thousand talers?

WERNER, *regaining his good temper at once*. Tomorrow, sir, tomorrow.

TELLHEIM. I no longer need to become your debtor, but I will become your banker. You good-natured people all need a guardian. You're a sort of spendthrift . . . I'm afraid I made you angry a while ago, Werner.

WERNER. God bless my soul, you did! I shouldn't have been such a fool. Now I see it all. I really deserved a hundred strokes, and you can give them to me, as long as you aren't angry any more, sir.

TELLHEIM. Angry? (*Shaking his hand.*) Read in my eyes everything I cannot put into words . . . I'd like to see the man who has a finer girl and a better friend than I have! . . . Isn't that right, Franziska? (*Exits.*)

SCENE FIFTEEN

FRANZISKA *and* WERNER

FRANZISKA, *aside*. Yes, he is a good man. I'll never meet another like him. I have to admit it. (*Shyly and modestly coming up to* WERNER.) Sergeant major . . .

WERNER, *wiping his eyes*. Well?

FRANZISKA. Sergeant major . . .

WERNER. What do you want, little lady?

FRANZISKA. Look at me, sergeant major.

WERNER. I can't yet; I don't know what I've got in my eye.

FRANZISKA. Just look at me!

WERNER. I'm afraid I looked at you a bit too much already, little lady . . . All right, now I'm looking at you. What's the matter?

FRANZISKA. Sergeant major, don't you need a Mrs. Sergeant major?

WERNER. Are you serious, little lady?

FRANZISKA. Absolutely!

WERNER. Would you like to go to Persia with me?

FRANZISKA. Wherever you like!

WERNER. Really? Hey, major, don't boast! I've got a girl who's at least as good as yours and a friend who's just as honest! . . . Give me your hand, little lady . . . Done! . . . In ten years you'll either be a general's wife or a widow.

Curtain